SUBSTANCE ABUSE, OPIOIDS

CRISIS, ADDICTION, AND THE WAY OUT

MILTON HARRISON

CONTENTS

Milton Harrison

NEED HELP ??
HERE IS A LIST OF A FEW OF THE TOP TREATMENT
SPECIALISTS IN THE COUNTRY

THE LIST INCLUDES:

- *Nationally renowned treatment providers*
- *One-click linked portal access*
- *Locations and contact information*
- *Things to remember when seeking or providing help*

It's one thing to need help, and another to know where to go......

To receive your Renowned Treatment List, visit the link:

Renowned Treatment List

INTRODUCTION

"One of the hardest things was learning that I was worth recovery."

— DEMI LOVATO

The relentless desire for self-gratification is, without a doubt, one of the most striking characteristics of modern society. Since we live in a world that glorifies instant pleasure over hard work and discipline, it is no secret that our society places very little value in the virtues of integrity, self-drive, and personal fulfillment. This obsession with self-indulgence has completely overtaken our innate desire for self-development and personal achievement, thereby leaving us empty and bereft of happiness. Consequently, many people resort to the use of various substances in a bid to get an "instant fix" and feel better about themselves. The result is an engineered drug crisis that has destroyed the lives of many promising individuals who would otherwise be effective assets in our society.

While most people get involved with drugs as a means of

escape from the pressures and anxieties of life, they quickly realize that these substances do not provide permanent relief or solutions to the problems that confront them.

Obviously, there is a temporary sense of comfort that these substances provide. This is often a facade, however, that quickly dissipates as soon as the effects of the drug wear off. Nevertheless, during the state of euphoria - which is aroused by the influence of these substances - most people fail to realize the risks and dangers that these drugs present, key of which is addiction.

The problem of substance dependency and addiction is one that has ravaged the lives of millions of people and continues to do so to many more. Medical studies have revealed that at least 40 million Americans aged 12 and older - more than 1 in 7 people - abuse or are addicted to nicotine, alcohol, or other drugs. This number is significantly higher than that of Americans suffering from heart conditions, diabetes, and cancer. Drug addiction is considered a major health crisis not only in America but throughout the world. That is why many governments are adopting increasingly radical measures in a bid to fight this scourge.

Generally, the drugs that have historically been known to contribute to high levels of addiction include marijuana and cocaine. In recent years, however, opioids such as oxycodone have become more central in the global drug crisis. This is mainly attributed to the ease with which these drugs can be acquired.

Furthermore, there is a lack of awareness of the side effects of these substances leading many people to wrongly assume that they are harmless. This misconception couldn't be further from the truth.

According to the US Department of Health and Human Services, more than 130 people died everyday from opioid-related overdoses between the years 2016 and 2017. Reports also showed that opioid-related fatalities accounted for more than half of all drug overdoses in the same year. These statistics undoubtedly paint a very grim picture of the drug crises that have ravaged the world.

If you have fallen victim to substance abuse, you may feel like all hope is lost and that you've sunk too low to pull yourself out of your drug problem. This is not necessarily the case. By making a bold decision and applying the right strategies, you can overcome the problem of opioid addiction and reclaim your health and productivity. Obviously, getting rid of any kind of addiction can be extremely challenging. But with the right state of mind and a genuine resolve, you can completely let go of your addiction problem and come out of the other side a clean, whole, and healthy individual. It is never too late to give up the self-destructive habit of drug use and abuse, and in doing so, improve your overall quality of life in a major way.

Over the course of my long and illustrious career as a self-help author and speaker, I have encountered many individuals who have suffered from opioid addiction and observed the toll it took on their lives. I spent a number of years immersed in extensive research in this area and worked closely with individuals and organizations that have helped broaden my knowledge on opioid addiction. Through scientific study and anecdotal evidence, I have compiled a comprehensive manual on how to completely overcome drug addiction and improve your quality of life. I am very pleased by the positive reviews I have received from people who have applied my method, and in doing so, managed to beat their opioid addiction. I have no doubt whatsoever that the wisdom contained in this book will be a great resource in the battle with drug addiction.

Some of the important lessons that I cover in this book include:

- The specific human experiences that contribute to opioid addiction
- The **two treacherous faces of opioids,** and why you need to be careful
- The 5 things you should always ask your doctor before taking any narcotics
- The **3 risk factors** that very few people are aware of when it comes to opiates
- Reasons that push people to use drugs, and how to get them to stop
- The top **signs of addiction you SHOULDN'T miss** to protect your loved ones
- How to be **quick and alert** in responding to withdrawal symptoms and **avoid a fatal** overdose

While drug addiction is a serious cause for concern, you need not get overly anxious or worried even if you are particularly affected by this scourge. By maintaining the right mindset, you will be able to garner the strength you need to completely beat the opioid problem and start living a healthier life today.

It is also important to note that addiction is an illness like any other, and the people affected by it deserve love and compassion rather than judgment. Adopting this kind of attitude will allow you to see the problem for what it is and consequently learn how to confront it in productive ways that will guarantee success.

1

THE UNAVOIDABLE HUMAN EXPERIENCE

E veryone has experienced pain in one form or another at some point in their lives. It is not too far-fetched to assume that every human being is (to some degree) familiar with the concept of pain. Pain is an integral part not only of our individual perception, but also of our collective human experience.

The science behind pain has been shrouded by mystery despite the universal nature of this condition. Humans throughout history have come up with different theories to explain the existence of pain and the role it plays in our lives. It is only in the past three centuries, however, that scientists and philosophers have developed insights into the nature of pain and devised effective ways of managing it in all its forms.

In this opening chapter, we are going to begin by defining what pain is and embark on an in-depth exploration of its multifaceted nature. Some of the key subjects that we are going to look at include the common perceptions of pain as it manifests in our subjective life experiences as well as the different types of pain human beings encounter. Furthermore, this chapter will provide a brief history of pain management in order to set a background for a study of modern pain relief practices and techniques. Finally, we will look at the correlation between pain and substance abuse which will set the tone for the subsequent chapters of this book.

Commonly Held Conceptions of Pain

Since the dawn of mankind, pain has been a dominant condition and an overarching aspect of the human experience. Ancient civilizations had different conceptions of pain, which guided their understanding of it and the kind of actions they sought to provide relief. Until recently, however, the nature of pain was not well understood. For the purposes of this book, it is important for us to define what pain is and the different ways in which it is perceived.

Pain is fundamentally a primal sensation belonging to a class known as bodily sensations. Other bodily sensations that belong in the same category include tingles, orgasms, and itches. Pain, like all other bodily sensations, is localized in specific parts of one's body at any given time. In addition to this, the sensation of pain is characterized by a distinct intensity and duration relative to certain physical objects (body organs in this case). Another feature of pain that is shared by other bodily sensations is its intimate or subjective nature, meaning that only the individual afflicted by pain is privy to all of its attributes, including its intensity and duration.

This multidimensional nature of pain has led many thinkers and scientists to draw a paradoxical conclusion about pain, namely that it is both a physical object present in the body and simultaneously a metaphysical self-intimating condition that is impossible to quantify. As we are going to see in subsequent chapters of this book, pain straddles both physical and non-physical reality in a very complicated relationship between the body and the mind.

The commonly held conception of pain is one that everyone is familiar with largely because of its epistemic immediacy. In this conception of pain, there are two threads that appear to pull in different directions, thereby giving rise to an act-object duality, which informs our ordinary experience and perception of pain.

In the first thread of commonly held perceptions, pain is regarded as a specific condition of particular body parts or organs. This perception of pain is typically reflected in a localized description of pain. For instance, when one says, "I have an ache in my left shoulder," or, "I feel a sharp pain in my left thumb," one is describing pain as a specific condition of certain localized body parts or organs. In this example, pain is described using straightforward perceptual statements.

This understanding of pain essentially treats the characteristics of pain as if they're the objects of our perceptions. They also prompt us to focus our attention on those specific body locations in a bid to relieve the pain or reduce its intensity. If you have a toothache, for example, you will take the necessary measures to get rid of the pain either through medication or other types of treatment.

While the commonly held conception of pain seems to point to a localized description of pain, it paradoxically stops short of attributing the pain to a physical object or condition. Although one may feel the sensation of pain in a specific part of their body, they do not perceive it as arising from a specific object within the body part. This resistance of attributing pain to a physical object inside the body is informed by the second thread of our commonly held conception of pain, namely, that pain is a subjective experience.

As a subjective experience, pains are considered to be experiences in themselves rather than objects of perceptual experience. This commonly held perception of pain is more dominant and almost universally regarded as the scientific definition of pain, By following this thread of thought, pain can be described as an unpleasant sensation or emotional experience that arises out of intense or damaging stimuli. It is, however, important to note that pain, by its very definition, is subjective in nature and a person's understanding of this phenomenon is shaped by their unique experiences of injury in the early stages of their lives.

The subjective commonly held conception of pain encapsulates both the physical sensation that is brought about by injury as well as the inevitable emotional experience that follows from it. In order for a certain experience to qualify as painful, there has to be an unpleasant sensation as well as an emotional response. In this subjective conception, pain is always considered as a psychological state rather than an actual physical object within a localized body part of an individual. This, as you can see, is in sharp contrast to the first conception, which regards pain as being purely descriptive of a specific physical condition with distinctive spatio-temporal characteristics.

When we describe our experiences of pain, we normally talk about 'feeling' them. The implication is that they are physical objects inside our bodies and we are privy to them through inner perception that is largely due to the private and self-intimating nature of this phenomenon. Furthermore, it points to the intricate way in which our physical bodies are connected to our mental processes. The quality of pain, being a private affair, means that no one can have knowledge of or access to the pain of another individual apart from the individual who is experiencing the pain and expressing it. Even two people who are subjected to the same unpleasant sensation, for instance, two terminally ill cancer patients, will each have unique insights and perceptions of the pain.

Pain is also considered to be subjective because it depends on the perception of an individual for its existence. In other words, pain cannot exist unless it is 'felt' by an individual. Very often, when we express our sympathy to other people for their painful experiences, we tend to say that we "feel their pain." While this is not morally wrong or unethical, it is fundamentally incorrect. Only the individual who is afflicted by the unpleasant sensations that arise from injury or damage and the mental discomfort that comes with it can claim any real authority on their pain. In the same breath, only the people who are directly affected by pain can provide infallible reports about their experience of the same.

The self-intimating nature of pain makes it impossible for there to be a disconnect between the appearance of pain and the reality of it. This means as long as an individual is in the same psychological situation that they would be in if they were in pain, then they are in pain. Conversely, if a person is faced with the same psychological situation that they would have in the absence of pain, then they are not in pain. Since there is no distinction between the appearance of pain and its reality, it is highly unlikely or even impossible for an individual to be mistaken in their judgments of their own pain.

TYPES OF PAIN

Now that we have demystified the commonly held conception of pain, let us look at the main categories of pain that we usually encounter as human beings. Notably, pain can be categorized into three main types: nociceptive pain, neuropathic pain, and psychogenic pain.

Nociceptive Pain

Nociceptive pain is by-and-large the most common type of pain that we experience as human beings. It arises when harmful stimuli are detected by pain receptors known as nociceptors. Nociceptors typically register pain in case a body part is affected by injury or physical damage. This includes injuries such as cuts, bruises, and fractures. Nociceptors are also able to detect thermal and chemical damage.

When there is an injury to a certain part of the body, the nociceptors are stimulated and they promptly send electric signals to the brain through the central nervous system. The brain then processes the information and perceives it as pain; this helps to protect the affected area from further harm or damage.

Nociceptive pain can be classified as chronic or acute, depending on the cause of the pain and its intensity. Most chronic illnesses such as cancer and arthritis often cause recurrent pain which may render a victim incapacitated. Since some of these medical conditions are untreatable, the pain is usually mitigated or suppressed through palliative care with the help of opiates such as morphine.

Nociceptive pain is also commonly classified as either somatic or visceral pain. Somatic pain originates from the nociceptors that are found on the surface of the body and in musculoskeletal tissues. This type of nociceptive pain can be experienced on the skin, tissue, and muscles. Most somatic pains tend to be localized to specific parts of the body and often get worse during physical activities. The pain can, however, be significantly eased through rest.

Visceral pain, on the other hand, arises when the receptors of internal body tissues and organs are activated as a result of injury or damage. Unlike somatic pain which is localized, visceral pain is usually vague, meaning it is difficult to pinpoint any specific part of the body where it arises. This type of pain is often described as a feeling of pressure or ache in the pelvis or abdomen. Some of the events that may trigger visceral pain include distention of hollow organs such as intestines and contraction of visceral muscles. Mild cases of visceral pain can be relieved using over-the-counter painkillers. In cases where significant organ damage has occurred, however, more serious treatments such as surgeries may be required.

Neuropathic Pain

This is a type of pain that is perceptible even when the affected area is exposed to non-painful stimuli. Moreover, it can manifest continuously or in the form of paroxysms. Some of the common features of neuropathic pain in the affected area may include a burning feeling or coldness, itching, and sharp prickly sensations.

The main cause of neuropathic pain is nerve damage that can be caused by an illness such as diabetes, viral infections, and in some cases, surgical procedures. This type of pain is often very difficult to treat and most people only end up achieving some form of partial relief. Nevertheless, there are several treatments that can be recommended to an individual who is experiencing extreme neuropathic pain. These include anticonvulsants such as pregabalin and gabapentin, as well as opioid analgesics.

Psychogenic Pain

Unlike the previous types of pain, psychogenic pain is not an official diagnostic term for pain. The term is, however, commonly used descriptively for pain that is caused or aggravated by mental disturbances such as stress, anxiety, and depression. Some of the common examples of psychogenic pain include headaches, stomach pains, and backaches.

This pain is usually caused by emotional events such as grief, heartbreak, and lovesickness. In some people, it may also be triggered by mental disorders such as bipolar disorder and depression.

Psychogenic pain is often a subject of controversy since there are no physical, sensory damages that are attributed to it. Many people consider it as unreal, thereby stigmatizing the sufferers of this type of pain. Nevertheless, some experts on the subject believe that the purpose of psychogenic pain is to provide a distraction so that extreme emotions which have been suppressed in the subconscious do not surface.

A BRIEF HISTORY OF PAIN MANAGEMENT

Throughout history, humans of all civilizations have sought to find ways to soothe pain or cure it completely. In most ancient societies, pain was generally regarded as a punishment inflicted on humans by the gods for their misdemeanors. To appease the gods and soften their wrath, humans often conducted rituals, which included some kind of animal sacrifice being offered up as atonement. In other cultures, such as the American Indians, various kinds of paraphernalia such as gongs and rattles were used to chase away spirits believed to cause pain inside a person's body.

As primitive forms of medicine began to evolve, healers started using more enhanced, albeit crude forms of treatment to soothe pain. One of the most common techniques that was adopted as a pain-relief mechanism is trepanation. This involved drilling a small hole through a patient's skull to get rid of pain arising from migraines, intracranial diseases, and other serious cranial injuries. While the effectiveness of this procedure in curing pain is largely unknown today, the fact that it was practiced in several cultures, including the Incas and Greeks, suggests that it enjoyed a reasonable degree of success.

Other ancient civilizations pioneered pain-relief techniques and treatments that would later be adopted by modern societies. Ancient Egyptian healers, for instance, were known for fetching electric eels from the Nile and placing them over the wounds of their patients to relieve their pain. A modern version of this pain-relief method (also known as transcutaneous electric nerve stimulation) is used today to treat arthritis pains and backaches.

The use of plant-based remedies to treat pain became popular in Medieval times. A wide variety of herbs was used to cure all sorts of pains, including those arising from underlying health conditions and injuries. In most cases, the herbal medicines contained dozens of different compounds, including opiates.

During the 19th and early 20th centuries, various treatments emerged involving the use of magnets and electricity to treat pain. These treatments were more often than not devised by quacks who were too eager to make some quick money from the gullibility of others. At the same time, there were other commercially available remedies that contained varying amounts of opiates or alcohol. These types of treatment were used particularly to provide temporary relief for pain during medical procedures.

The first significant development in pain relief and treatment came in 1846 when William T.G Morton, a dentist from Boston, and John Collins Warren, a surgeon, performed the first successful surgery with anesthesia. This achievement was an important milestone because it eradicated the pain of surgery, which had been one of mankind's biggest fears. Since then, millions of successful surgical procedures have been performed throughout the world and anesthesia has become a key element of modern surgical practice.

PAIN AND SUBSTANCE ABUSE

Chronic pain can be a very debilitating condition for anyone. It can strain your mobility and hinder your ability to work or exercise. Being in constant pain can also affect your mental state and contribute to illnesses such as depression and anxiety. It is not surprising that many people who are afflicted by chronic pain are at high risk of substance abuse.

Most individuals often turn to drugs as a means of alleviating the pain they are experiencing. For those who are already struggling with substance addiction, the use of medicine to soothe pain can be a very complicated process. Some may turn to alcohol and other drugs such as opiates to find relief for their pain. While drugs and alcohol may provide temporary distractions from pain, they are not very effective in the long run and may even be more damaging to the individual than the actual pain that they are trying to mitigate.

Substance abuse can interfere with one's sleeping patterns

and exacerbate mental problems such as anxiety and depression. If the dependency on drugs is not checked, it can wreak havoc on an individual's personal life and mess up their careers. Frequent drug users may also find it difficult to take care of themselves and their families. This can negatively affect their relationships with their loved ones and worsen their situation further.

The treatment of chronic pain, in itself, can also contribute to serious drug dependency issues and addiction. Most doctors often prescribe opiate medications such as Oxycodone and Hydrocodone for pain relief. While the chances of developing an addiction to these drugs is quite low, it is by no means non-existent. Patients who have a history of addiction are particularly at risk of developing a dependency on these drugs. Even those who have no prior history can still become addicted to these drugs due to the fact that they are easily accessible. Moreover, it is easy for patients to exceed the recommended dose due to a desperate need for relieving their chronic pain. This can significantly heighten the risk of developing an addiction to these opioid medications.

The fact that these drugs often induce a 'high' mental state and a calming effect on the body usually prompts patients to seek them out in order to relive that experience. As a result, they become addicted to that feeling and end up dependent on these drugs to function in their ordinary lives.

In light of these concerns, some medical practitioners and primary care physicians have been compelled to find alternative methods of pain management to alleviate their patients' chronic pain. Some of the options that have been suggested include non-drug pain relief methods such as acupuncture, chiropractic treatment, and mind-body therapies. These treatments are highly effective when it comes to the management of chronic pain, and are also considered much safer than opioid medications.

Obviously, there are instances where opiate-based drugs may be more beneficial for chronic pain management. Due to their high risk for addiction, these medicines should only be used when necessary under the advice and supervision of qualified physicians. Patients who have a history of addiction can also use opioid medications for their chronic pain as long as the prescribed treatment takes into account the necessary measures to address their safety and risk of abuse. Otherwise, they risk relapsing back to substance abuse, which can erode any progress that they may have made in their recovery journey.

PAIN CAN BE CONSTRUCTIVE, TOO

Pain is often a very unpleasant experience. Being in constant pain can severely affect our physical, mental, and emotional wellbeing. Pain can hinder us from living our lives to their fullest potential. It is no surprise that our immediate reaction to pain is to find ways of soothing it or eliminating it completely.

Having the mindset of pain as something completely 'negative' can hinder us from understanding the multifaceted nature of pain, and prevent us from deriving any value from our experiences. Despite its negative implications to our physical and emotional wellbeing, pain can actually be beneficial to us in a number of ways.

One of the main benefits of pain is that it enables us to develop empathy for others. For instance, painful experiences such as terminal illness, mental distress, and personal loss can force us to investigate the dynamics of our lives and put into perspective the scope of our human experience. Through these experiences, we come to the realization that despite our minute differences like cultural background, nationality, education, and profession, the existential problems that confront us are the same. Pain teaches us that at the very core of our humanity, we are all the same and that the various things that separate us, such as race, tribe, and religion, are merely illusions. Thanks to the wisdom that we receive through our experiences of pain, we naturally develop a sense of solidarity with our fellow men and women.

Another key benefit of pain is that it motivates us to establish the support structures and defense systems that are essential to our survival. While physical pain is often an indicator of possible tissue damage, it can also be a sign of harmful lifestyle practices. Smoking, for instance, can lead to chest pains due to lung congestion and serious respiratory problems. Likewise, failure to observe a healthy diet and exercise can lead to unhealthy body weight and cause physical pain due to strain on the joints and muscles. While it is always good to take preemptive measures to safeguard our health, sometimes the pain that we experience can be the wake-up call that we need to change our lifestyles and start living better.

Similarly, the emotional and psychological pain that we experience due to unhealthy relationships and loneliness can force us to re-evaluate ourselves and identify the problems that are holding us back. In doing so, we can learn from our mistakes and adopt healthy habits and practises that enable us to build meaningful and satisfying relationships with others. This will help you achieve a greater sense of peace, contentment, and wellbeing.

Another possible benefit of pain is that it helps in character development. Notably, the experience of pain, by virtue of its unpleasantness, pushes us to the limits of our being. This can be a very uncomfortable and distressing thing to go through, that is why most people tend to despair when they are afflicted by pain. Maintaining a positive attitude even when faced with chronic pain and adversity can allow you to develop virtues such as perseverance, patience, and self-discipline. It can also teach us to be more restrained with our desires and appetite, thereby making us mentally stronger and more resilient individuals.

It is important to remember that pain is temporary and transient. No kind of pain, regardless of how chronic it might be, lasts forever. By adopting a positive mindset towards pain, you will be able to muster the strength needed to deal with the discomfort with the hope that one day it shall all pass. Doing so will empower you to persevere through your pain and emerge from the other side as a better person.

In summary, here are some of the main takeaways from this chapter:

- Pain is an indicator of tissue damage and an important bodily sensation that alerts us of physical danger.
- The sensation of pain has a physical component as well as an emotional response.
- Pain is a highly subjective experience; its existence depends on the perception of an individual.
- The experience of pain can be constructive because it allows one to build their character and to develop important virtues such as perseverance, empathy, and patience.

2

ADDICTION AND STIGMA

Whether physical, emotional or psychological, pain can be a very difficult problem to deal with. Normally, when most people experience pain, they look for various ways to try and mitigate it. One of the strategies that they may adopt is the use of prescription opioids to manage or soothe their pain. While the use of opioid drugs may provide temporary relief from pain, this habit often leads to the problems of dependence and addiction, which can take a serious toll on one's health and life.

When we discuss the problem of addiction, we look at how it emerges and progresses, and why it is such a big problem when it comes to effective pain management. More importantly, we will look at the stigma that surrounds and labels addiction and why it is harmful to individuals who are trying to quit taking drugs. We will also cover some of the best strategies of combating addiction stigma in order to create a safe and supportive environment for those trying to quit drugs.

REASONS WHY PEOPLE START TAKING DRUGS

There are numerous factors that make certain people more predisposed to drug-taking. These include:

Genetic Factors

Genetics often plays a role in shaping people's preferences for drugs. Moreover, the interaction between genetics and social factors can make some individuals more predisposed to drug use than others. Children of alcoholic parents, for example, are at a much higher risk of alcohol use and abuse.

Cultural Norms

An individual's preference for drugs is often shaped by the cultural norms and values of the society in which they live. In much of the western world, for instance, the use of drugs and alcohol in universities and colleges is a well-known phenomenon and most campuses lack stringent policies to control their use.

Financial Means

Studies have shown that there is a relationship between financial ability and propensity for drug-taking. For instance, states that have lenient tax laws on drugs usually have higher numbers of drug users. Similarly, states that have higher taxes on drugs such as cigarettes and alcohol tend to have reduced rates of alcoholism and drug-taking.

Self-Medication

Individuals who suffer from chronic pain are often required to take opiate-based prescription drugs to relieve the pain. Even though these drugs are prescribed by a doctor, the resulting addiction and drug dependency cases make it very difficult for those addicted to function without the use of their prescription. Likewise, some people resort to taking alcohol and drugs such as marijuana to cope with emotional and psychological pain.

Personal Temperament

The propensity for drug use is closely related to the personality of an individual. In essence, people who are impulsive by nature tend to value immediate gratification more than delayed rewards, and are likely to take drugs to chase the 'high' feeling without considering the long-term risks involved.

EFFECTS OF DRUG ABUSE ON THE BODY AND BRAIN

Drugs are chemical substances that can have tremendous effects on one's body and psychological state. Most drugs usually have long-lasting health implications, and their effects can be seen long after one has stopped taking them. Although some drugs can have positive health benefits, others can be very damaging to one's mental state. This is especially true if the drugs are used contrary to the recommendation of a physician.

Here are some of the effects of drug abuse:

- Suppressed immunity and increased risk of illness
- Increased risk of heart conditions and possible heart failure
- Lack of appetite due to nausea, which can lead to weight loss
- Lung disease, especially if one has been in taking the drugs by smoking
- Increased chances of having seizures and strokes

- Poor memory and problems with decision-making

The most severe effect of drug abuse on the body is death, which often occurs due to overdose. In the US alone, it is estimated that at least 100 people die every day due to opioid-related overdose.

Apart from their negative implications on physical health, drugs also have tremendous effects on the brain and mental health. Notably, drugs such as marijuana, cocaine, and heroin affect the brain's reward mechanism, which is connected to the limbic system. The use of these drugs usually causes large amounts of dopamine (*a chemical that regulates mood and feelings of pleasure*) to be released in the brain, and this triggers the 'high' feeling.

Although most people don't anticipate the possibility of getting addicted, the feeling that drugs induce often leads people to get hooked on them. That's why many victims of drug abuse often go to great extremes to get a 'quick fix.'

Common drugs such as alcohol and marijuana can have both short-term and long-term effects on the brain. Alcohol, for example, interferes with the brain's communication pathways, and can cause drastic changes in one's mood. Marijuana, on the other hand, causes short term memory loss.

Similarly, drug and substance abuse can affect an individual, both in the short term and long term. Some of the effects of substance abuse include:

- Increased paranoia and anxiety
- Aggressive impulses
- Visual and auditory hallucinations
- Impaired judgment
- Lack of self-control

Regular intake of drugs can also lead to addiction if it is not controlled early enough. People who become addicted to drugs usually find it difficult to function without taking the substances that they are addicted to. This is why giving up drugs can be a huge challenge for most people. Due to lack of awareness, people tend to demonize drug users and castigate them for taking drugs when, in fact, the drug users are themselves victims of drugs. By understanding how addiction works, and why it is such a huge challenge, we can change our attitude towards victims of substance abuse and become more compassionate towards and supportive of them.

ADDICTION IS A DISEASE

In most societies, drug addiction is perceived to be a moral weakness. As a result, drug addicts are often seen as careless and treated with contempt. The fact of the matter is that drug and substance addiction is a disease rather than a person's moral failing. When people start taking drugs, they usually do so with the belief that they are able to control their usage. As they continue taking them, their brains undergo significant changes, and their bodies gradually build up a tolerance for the drug. When this happens, the individual can no longer achieve their desired feeling from their normal intake of these substances. As a result, they begin taking higher amounts of the drugs to achieve the 'high' they are looking for.

Eventually, the chemical changes that are happening in the brain trigger the impulsive and uncontrollable urge to take drugs, and the individuals become addicted. Once this happens, the person is unable to voluntarily choose not to take drugs even if they are aware of the negative effects that the drug is having on their health and wellbeing.

As you already know, addiction typically occurs when a person's brain chemistry has been altered by habitual drug use. Individuals who manifest chronic addiction often find it very difficult to stop using drugs, and can relapse many times when they try to quit. Abstinence from drugs during this stage can cause serious withdrawal effects, and makes it very hard for addicts to stop taking drugs. In light of this, it is important for drug addiction to be treated as an illness that requires patients to be provided with intensive treatment and support.

People who consider addiction not to be a disease often believe that the problem originates from an individual's life choices. While this might be the case, it is not an entirely truthful or comprehensive assessment. Although a person may have control over their use of drugs (in the initial stages), once they become addicted, they may end up acting in ways that go against their values and beliefs.

Other individuals insist that addiction is not a disease, simply because it can be treated by abstaining from drugs. This could not be further from the truth. For most drug addicts, the effects of abstaining from drugs can be far more serious and dangerous than taking them. In order to rehabilitate themselves from drugs, users are required to go through intensive treatment and lifelong management, similar to people who suffer from chronic conditions such as diabetes and arthritis.

Drug addiction, just like any other illness, usually comes with its own fair share of symptoms. Some of the signs of addiction include:

- Extreme weight loss or gain
- Significant changes in appearance and body hygiene

- Dilated pupils
- Poor psychomotor coordination
- Slurred speech
- Drastic and unexpected changes in mood
- Increased irritability
- Lack of interest and motivation

Due to the lack of understanding about drug and substance abuse, many victims are often stigmatized and treated with contempt. This further exacerbates the use of drugs, since the users may feel isolated and cast-out. In order to help people who are addicted to drugs, a change of mindset is very important. In essence, drug abuse should be treated as an illness that can be cured with the right strategies and support.

FACTORS THAT CONTRIBUTE TO DRUG ADDICTION

Addiction is a very individualistic illness that can be brought about by a number of factors. Some of the main issues that contribute to substance abuse and addiction include:

Trauma

The traumatic events that an individual goes through in their lives often play a role in catalyzing an addiction problem. People who have undergone traumas such as neglect, abuse, and accidents are likely to turn to drugs as a means to ease their pain.

Mental Illness

Studies have shown a strong correlation between mental illness and substance abuse. Most individuals who take drugs usually do so to relieve themselves of stress, anxiety, and feelings of hopelessness that they feel. Conversely, the use of drugs can trigger mental illness or even exacerbate any pre-existing mental problems that one may be suffering from.

Environment

The environment in which one is brought up in can also contribute to substance abuse later in life. Children who are raised by parents who fight a lot, for instance, may resort to drug use to cope with the feelings of anger and neglect that they are experiencing. Similarly, individuals who are brought up by parents who use drugs may be inclined to start taking drugs themselves due to a normalized perception of drugs.

Pressure and Influence from Peers

While peer pressure is usually associated with children and teenagers, adults can also fall victim to the influence of people around them. If one spends time around friends who take drugs, for instance, they can be lured into doing the same as a way of bonding. This can lead to drug abuse and, subsequently, addiction.

FIGHTING ADDICTION STIGMA

Addiction stigma refers to the negative perceptions and beliefs that people hold about drug addicts. Studies have shown that stigma contributes to mental health problems in victims of drug abuse and addiction, and can interfere with their lifestyle. This means any form of discrimination and prejudice can negatively affect their self-esteem, damage their relationships with other people, and even hinder them from accessing treatment. In some cases, the stigma can drive them to commit suicide.

Addiction stigma is often perpetrated by friends and family

of the victims of drug abuse. They may judge the person harshly and use dehumanizing terms such as 'junkie' and 'crackhead' to denigrate them. People who do this often wrongly assume that the individual struggling with addiction is irresponsible. They may even be inclined to conclude that the person enjoys being in that condition. This perception could not be further from the truth. Drug addiction, as we have seen, is a serious disease that robs the victim of the ability to make rational choices. Individuals who are struggling with drug addiction need to be accorded support, understanding, and love, instead of judgment and prejudice.

Most individuals who perpetrate stigma against victims of drug addiction often don't realize the damaging effects their habits have on people who are trying to quit drugs. The stigma can have very serious social and emotional implications on individuals affected by addiction. They may feel isolated, marginalized, and lonely, and this can lead to problems such as depression and can increase the potential for self-harm and suicide.

Constant discrimination may also cause victims of drug use to conceal their problems and avoid seeking help. This can further exacerbate the problem and fuel their drug use. When individuals are stigmatized by society due to their drug addiction, they may get stuck in a cycle of drug abuse. In order to help addiction victims overcome their unhealthy habits, it is important to get rid of all stigma that is associated with substance abuse. The question remains: how can we achieve this?

We need to be more open about drug addiction, recovery, and treatment. Granted, talking about addiction can be an uncomfortable experience, especially if a close ally is the victim. Speaking about these difficult problems, however, can help us to personify it and start empathizing with the victims.

We can also end the stigma surrounding addiction by changing the language we use when speaking about it. In our society, drug addiction is often considered as an outcome of poor decision making, and victims are often tagged with demeaning terms such as 'loser' or 'druggie.' This can seriously damage their self worth and confidence, and make them feel hopeless. Instead of chastising drug addicts using these derogatory terms, it is more prudent to address the problem of addiction as a disease that anyone can be afflicted by.

Similarly, we can cast aside stigma by encouraging those who struggle with drug abuse to seek professional treatment. Unfortunately, we live in a world where asking for help is often seen as a weakness. As mentioned before, this can discourage individuals who struggle with addiction from speaking about their situation. By changing our mindset about addiction, however, we can begin to see drug abuse as a serious health problem, thus incentivizing victims to seek treatment.

A lot still remains to be done when it comes to handling addiction stigma. By changing our perception about drug use and abuse, we can let go of the misconceptions we hold and become more inclined towards treatment and recovery.

This chapter has certainly provided valuable insights into the nature of addiction and the stigma around it. As we conclude this segment, here are some of the key takeaways that we would do well to keep in mind:

- Addiction is a disease that requires professional treatment. Victims should be treated with empathy and provided with the support they need on their journey to recovery.

- There are several factors that may contribute to drug abuse and addiction. These include environmental factors, genetic factors, traumas, and mental health issues.
- Stigma from family, friends, and society can be very damaging to the mental wellbeing of individuals who are struggling with drugs, and this stigma can hinder them from seeking treatment.
- Changing our perceptions about drug addiction can help the fight against stigma and motivate victims to seek the help they need to recover. This will help avoid fatalities and extreme cases of opioid addiction.

3

OPIOIDS AND WHY BE SKEPTICAL

F or nearly two decades, the U.S. has been embroiled in a serious opioid crisis that has, to date, claimed hundreds of thousands of lives. The staggering number of deaths related to opioid overdose prompted the Health and Human Services (HHS) to declare a national health emergency and announce various strategies to mitigate the crisis.

Opium, the drug from which opioids are derived, became available in the United States in 1775. During the civil war in the 1860s, the drug was mainly used to treat injured soldiers. As a result, 400,000 soldiers (who had been given morphine) became addicted. By the late 1800s, the rate of opioid addiction had increased significantly due to the over-the-counter availability of opioids. In the early 1900s, morphine became the most commonly prescribed drug for pain management. At the same time, many people started using opioid drugs recreationally, by crushing the pills and inhaling them.

In order to limit the recreational use of opioid drugs, the Harrison Narcotics Act made opioids available only by prescription. In the years beginning 1920 to 1950, opioids were exclusively prescribed to patients who were dying for their acute pain rather than chronic pain. This was done in order to avoid addiction. By the early 1970s, there was a lot of stigma and fear associated with opioid addiction. As a result, doctors started to opt for surgery and other non-pharmaceutical treatment for chronic pain.

From 1970 to 1990, the American Pain Society advocated for the use of non-addictive therapies to treat cancer-related pain. The FDA also approved the use of Vicodin and Percocet for the decade starting 1976 to 1986. In 1986, however, the World Health Organization (WHO) created a set of guidelines to treat cancer patients. The organization recommended that opioids be used to treat chronic pain in cancer patients only if no other treatment options were available. Between the years 1997 to 2002, there was a sharp rise in the number of prescriptions for opioid drugs. Morphine prescriptions increased by 73% and hydromorphone by 96% whereas the prescriptions for fentanyl and Oxycodone spiked by 226% and 402% respectively.

By the mid-2000s, there were numerous reports of teenagers starting to use opioids obtained from their parent's prescriptions. Heroin also became available and started being used illicitly. In 2013, there were an estimated 23 000 drug-dependent babies who were born with Neonatal Abstinence Syndrome. Two years later, the number of reported opioid overdose deaths had increased to 52 404. Currently, the death rate from opioid overdose is 142 every single day.

The trajectory of opioid-related deaths can be documented in three phases. The first phase began in the early 1990s when pharmaceutical companies declared that patients would not become addicted to opioid prescription drugs. This provided an incentive for health providers to prescribe these drugs to patients. As a result, the number of opioid overdoses started increasing dramatically in the late 1990s.

The second phase of the opioid crisis started in 2010 when the use of heroin skyrocketed in the U.S. This led to a rapid increase in overdose-related deaths, which claimed thousands. In 2013, the opioid crisis entered its third phase with a significant increase in the number of opioid-related deaths involving illegal synthetic opioids such as fentanyl. The market for fentanyl has been steadily growing ever since despite government efforts to clamp down on the illegal drug trade.

The perpetuation of the opioid crisis has been mainly facilitated by a lack of information and awareness about these drugs and the dangers they pose. Pharmaceutical companies, for instance, have been complicit in this health crisis by downplaying the harmful effects of the drugs, and encouraging health providers to continue prescribing them.

Let us now explore the topic of opioids, what they are, and why they are very central to the health disaster that we've been facing for more than two decades.

What are Opioids?

Opioids are a class of drugs that are derived from the opium poppy plant. While most opioids are used as prescription drugs, some types of opioids are purely used for recreational purposes.

Opioids work by inhibiting the pain signals between the body and the brain. That's why they are usually administered as painkillers to patients who are suffering from chronic pain. These drugs can also induce a relaxing and calming 'high' feeling, which makes them highly addictive.

Opioids are commonly referred to as narcotics. This is because they don't belong in the same class as other painkillers like Tylenol and aspirin, even though they do have the same pain relief properties. Although these drugs are often prescribed for use by medical practitioners, they are not entirely safe. As a matter of fact, opioids tend to have very serious side effects.

Some of the short-term health effects of opioids include:

- Drowsiness
- Mental fog
- Constipation
- Shallow breathing
- Nausea
- Unconsciousness

Frequent use of prescription opioids can lead to increased tolerance and dependence. As a result, patients may find that they require higher quantities each time in order to achieve the desired effect. This can eventually lead to addiction, which is clinically referred to as 'opioid use disorder.'

When taken at very high doses, opioids can lead to breathing complications or even death. It is worth noting that the risk of respiratory distress is much higher for people who are taking opioids for the first time, and those that are using medications that are known to react with these drugs.

Due to the severity of the risks involved, opioids should only be used for pain relief in cases where no other type of treatment is available. In addition to this, you should only use opioids as directed by a qualified physician, and you need to inform them about any pre-existing medical conditions that you may have, as well as any other drugs you may be using.

Types of Opioids

While the term 'opioid' is generally used to describe different types of drugs that are derived from the opium poppy plant, drugs that fall under this category have various differences. As such, they are further grouped depending on how they are made or acquired. Under this classification criterion, there are three categories of opioids, namely: Semi-synthetic opioids, fully synthetic opioids, and natural opiates.

Semi-synthetic opioids are a class of drugs that are manufactured artificially in medical labs using opiate compounds. Some of the well-known examples of these man-made opioids include drugs such as hydrocodone, oxycodone, and hydromorphone.

Unlike semi-synthetic opioids, which are made using opiate compounds, fully synthetic opioids are manufactured using other chemicals. Some of the drugs that fall in this category include fentanyl, tramadol, methadone, and pethidine.

Natural opiates are alkaloid compounds that occur naturally in the poppy plant. Some of the most common natural opiates include narcotine, codeine, morphine, papaverine, thebaine, and narceine.

Most naturally occurring and semi-synthetic opioids are legal and can be easily acquired from a pharmacy on the recommendations of a medical practitioner. These opioids are usually manufactured by pharmaceutical companies, which are strictly regulated by the government through certain safety standards. Synthetic opioids, on the other hand, are illegally made and sold by black market operators both locally and in foreign countries.

Since the manufacture and sale of synthetic opioid drugs are unregulated, many organizations and individuals who make them often mix harmful chemicals and drugs such as cocaine, methamphetamine, heroin, and MDMA. As a result, synthetic opioids are often far more dangerous and addictive than naturally occurring and semi-synthetic opioids. In fact, the past decade has seen a sharp rise in opioid-related fatalities, which are linked to illegal synthetic drugs such as fentanyl and methadone.

Nevertheless, the fact that prescription opioids such as oxycodone and hydrocodone are manufactured by licensed pharmaceutical companies does not necessarily mean that they are safe. These drugs have also contributed significantly to the opioid crisis and lead to many fatalities as a result of overdose. Some medical experts and observers even argue that these drugs are far more dangerous, owing to the fact that they are legal and easily accessible.

Given the tremendous risks that all the different types of opioids present to users, it is absolutely vital to be adequately informed on the dangers and side effects that these drugs may pose. Having the right information easily accessible can go a long way towards empowering individuals who are at high risk of addiction to make the right decisions when it comes to both legal and illegal opioids.

EFFECTS OF OPIOIDS ON THE BODY

As we have seen from the previous topic, opioids can be classified depending on how they are made. Using this criterion, we can categorize opioid drugs as naturally-occurring, semi-synthetic and fully synthetic. Depending on the manner in which they are derived and manufactured, different types of opioids will have different pharmacological effects.

In this section, we are going to look at the various effects that specific types of opioids have on the body. First, let us briefly go over some of the general effects that opioids tend to produce when ingested or administered:

Analgesic Effects

Opioids are mostly given to patients who are suffering from chronic pain because of the drug's strong analgesic effects. These drugs are highly effective at relieving poorly localized, dull pain that is emanating from deeper body structures such as muscles and organ tissues. Since neuropathic pain may be very persistent, patients often report that opioid medications help them manage it properly until it is almost unnoticeable in some cases. While opioids are quite effective at relieving neuropathic pain, however, they are ineffective when it comes to sharp nociceptive pain from injuries such as cuts on the skin.

Sedative Properties

Opioids are known to induce drowsiness and a relaxed feeling of tranquility. In some instances, the pain-relief properties of opioids are accompanied by sleep, although this is not always the case.

Euphoric and Dysphoric Feelings

Some opiates such as morphine and codeine often induce a feeling of euphoria and contentment when used. This feeling, accompanied by the pain-relief properties of the drugs, usually contributes to the addictive nature of these opioids. On the other hand, some opioids are known to elicit feelings of dysphoria. Even morphine, which is very effective as a pain-reliever, can cause restlessness and agitation in some patients when they realize they are no longer in pain.

Opioid Tolerance and Dependence

Although this phenomenon is not fully understood, many experts believe that increased tolerance to opioids may be as a result of a decrease in the production of endogenous opioids. These are the opioid compounds that are naturally released in the brain.

Another possible explanation for opioid tolerance is the downregulation of opioid receptors, which are responsible for mediating the body's response to different hormones and neurotransmitters.

Apart from increased tolerance, the habitual use of opioids can also lead to dependence - a condition whereby an individual experiences adverse physical symptoms whenever they withdraw from drug usage. Common symptoms that long-term opioid users may manifest include sweating, diarrhea, muscle cramps, vomiting, restlessness, and irritability.

Once a person develops a physical dependence, they may be unable to make rational choices about their drug use even when they are well aware of the implications on their health and wellbeing. This is why opioid dependence and addiction should be viewed and treated as the illness it is.

Rigidity of Muscles

When taken in very large doses, opioids may cause muscles to become more rigid and tense, especially around the thoracic cavity.

Suppressed Immunity

Prolonged opioid use puts the body under a lot of strain, and may lead to suppression of the body's immune system. This puts long-term users at great risk of contracting serious illnesses.

Although different opioids tend to produce similar effects,

they differ substantially in a number of ways, most notably, their duration of action. In order to truly appreciate how these drugs work, let us now look at the ways in which some of the most common opioids work.

Morphine

Morphine is a naturally occurring opioid medication that is derived from phenanthrene. It is perhaps the most well-known medicative opioid and is often considered the standard against which all other opioid drugs are measured.

Due to its effectiveness as a pain reliever, morphine is usually prescribed to persons that are suffering from chronic neuropathic pain. The drug can be administered in various ways including orally, intravenously, epidurally, and intramuscularly. Morphine typically has a quick onset of action, which peaks about 60 minutes after the injection has been administered. The drug also has a duration of action of 3-4 hours.

Some of the effects of morphine:

- Strong pain-relief and analgesic properties; that's why it is widely considered as the gold standard of opioid therapy.
- May induce euphoria, dysphoria, and hallucinations.
- Often causes respiratory depression by slowing down breathing.
- May induce nausea and vomiting.

Codeine

Codeine is a naturally occurring opiate and is often administered as a pain-relief medication. Although the actual mechanism of codeine is not fully understood, experts believe that it works by binding to the opioid receptors in the brain.

These receptors are responsible for transmitting the sensation of pain in the brain and body. Codeine, however, has a very low affinity for opioid receptors compared to other opioids like morphine and hydrocodone. Patients who take codeine often develop a high tolerance for their pain, although the sensation may still be apparent to them.

In addition to alleviating pain, codeine induces sedation and depresses breathing. The drug is also often combined with other drugs like aspirin and Tylenol to provide more effective pain relief.

Some of the side effects of codeine include:

- Euphoria
- Respiratory depression
- Dizziness
- Vomiting
- Constipation
- Abdominal pain
- Itching
- Rash
- Low blood pressure

Codeine, like all opioids, is an addictive drug. When used for pain relief over short periods of time, a dependency is unlikely although not entirely impossible. People who use the drug over prolonged periods may experience severe effects if the drug is suddenly withdrawn. This is why the dose of codeine should be reduced gradually, instead of sudden withdrawal.

Heroin

Heroin is an illegal opioid drug that is made from morphine, a naturally occurring substance found in the seedpods of certain varieties of the poppy plant. The drug is usually sold as a white or brownish powder or a black substance known as black tar heroin. This semi-synthetic drug is believed to be at least twice as potent as morphine, which makes it highly effective for pain management.

Heroin is usually administered or ingested in several different ways, including sniffing, snorting, and smoking. Once the drug reaches the brain, it is quickly converted into morphine, and rapidly binds to the opioid receptors.

Some of the immediate (short-term) side effects include:

- Drowsiness
- Sedation
- Nausea
- Vomiting
- Respiratory depression
- Slowed heart function

Studies have also shown that habitual heroin usage can affect a patient's brain and their ability to control their actions and make proper judgments.

Fentanyl

Fentanyl is a potent synthetic opioid, which is 50 to 100 times more potent than morphine. It is generally used as an analgesic to relieve chronic pain, especially from surgeries. The drug is also administered to patients experiencing chronic pain due to terminal illness.

Although fentanyl is treated as a prescription opioid, many illegal labs are known to manufacture the drug in the black market and sell it to users who have no doctor's prescription.

Some of the street names of fentanyl include China White, Apache, China Girl, Dance Fever, and Murder 8.

The illegal manufacture and sale of fentanyl has been central to the opioid crisis over the past decade. Statistics have shown that more than half of opioid-related fatalities are a result of a fentanyl overdose. People who ingest fentanyl in large doses are likely to experience hypoxia, a condition that reduces the amount of oxygen that reaches the brain. When this happens, users of the drug may suffer permanent brain damage or slip into a coma.

Some of the side effects of fentanyl include:

- Constipation
- Nausea
- Confusion
- Drowsiness
- Breathing problems
- Unconsciousness

Fentanyl overdoses are usually treated using a drug known as Naloxone. This drug acts by binding to the opioid receptors in the brain and inhibiting the action of opiates. Naloxone should be administered immediately after an overdose to inhibit fentanyl action and prevent serious brain damage and fatality. Since fentanyl is many times more potent than morphine or codeine, multiple doses of Naloxone are required to successfully treat fentanyl overdose.

Individuals who are given Naloxone should be closely monitored to ensure their breathing doesn't slow down or stop. The drug is typically administered as an injection or nasal spray.

Since fentanyl is a very addictive opioid, individuals who are hooked on the drug may find it difficult to stop using it. Moreover, sudden withdrawal of the drug may cause serious side effects such as:

- Diarrhea and vomiting
- Lack of sleep
- Uncontrollable body movements
- Severe cravings for fentanyl
- Muscle pain

Treatment for fentanyl usually involves medication and behavioral therapy. Some of the medicines that have been approved for treating fentanyl addiction include methadone and buprenorphine; both function by binding to the opioid receptors in the brain. This helps to reduce the patients' craving for fentanyl. Naltrexone, another commonly used drug, blocks opioid receptors in the brain, thus preventing fentanyl from binding to the brain's receptors.

In addition to medication, counseling is also very crucial in the treatment of fentanyl addiction, to help victims develop positive attitudes and practises in relation to their drug use.

Hydrocodone

Hydrocodone is a prescription opioid that is used to treat all types of pain. Unlike natural opiates like morphine and codeine, which occur naturally, hydrocodone is usually made in a lab. It is often administered to people who have serious injuries, or those that have undergone major procedures. Nevertheless, just like other opioids, hydrocodone is very addictive, and long-term use of the drug can lead to tolerance and dependence.

Some of the most commonly reported side effects of taking hydrocodone include:

- Reduced breathing rate
- Expanded pupils
- Sleepiness
- Slurred speech
- Vomiting
- Nausea
- Constipation
- Confusion
- Itchy skin
- Euphoria

Long-term use of hydrocodone can lead to lasting effects on the brain. Individuals who have developed an addiction for this drug may experience significant mood and behavioral changes. They are also likely to suffer from other health problems such as liver and kidney disease, respiratory stress, insomnia, anxiety, and depression.

Taking large amounts of hydrocodone can easily lead to an overdose. When this happens, the breathing rate of a user can plummet, thereby causing hypoxia (lack of enough oxygen reaching the brain). In severe cases of hydrocodone overdose, fatalities are likely to occur unless the patient receives immediate treatment.

Due to the serious health risks involved, hydrocodone should only be taken under the prescription of a medical professional.

Methadone

Methadone is often prescribed as a pain-relief medication, particularly to patients who have tolerance or adverse reactions to other opiates like morphine and codeine. More commonly, the drug is used to prevent withdrawal effects in patients who are going through treatment for opioid addiction.

It comes in various forms, including dispersible tablets, non-dispersible tablets, and concentrated solutions, and can either be administered orally or intravenously.

Some of the common side effects of methadone include:

- Drowsiness
- Slowed breathing
- Constipation
- Nausea
- Vomiting
- Headaches
- Abdominal Pain
- Dizziness

Although most mild side effects usually dissipate after a few days, the drug may cause more severe effects in some cases including respiratory failure and low blood pressure.

Some of the most common withdrawal effects that users of methadone are likely to experience include:

- Anxiety and irritability
- Restlessness
- Insomnia
- High blood pressure
- Increased breathing rate
- Fast heart rate
- Stomach cramps and diarrhea
- Muscle and back pains

Oxycodone

Oxycodone is a synthetic opioid drug that is commonly administered as a painkiller. It is also one of the most commonly abused prescription drugs in the U.S. Most people who abuse Oxycodone usually start out taking the prescribed dose. Then, as their tolerance with habitual use grows, they start requiring higher doses in order to experience the same effects.

The transition from prescriptive use to addiction can be very quick when it comes to Oxycodone. This is due to the high potency of the drug. Patients who are using it to manage pain due to chronic illnesses may find it difficult to control their use of the drug and end up becoming dependent. Some of the common signs and symptoms of Oxycodone dependence and addiction include:

- Requiring higher doses of the drug to achieve a high
- Experiencing unpleasant symptoms when Oxycodone is withdrawn
- Having intense cravings for the drug when not under the influence of it
- Prioritizing the drug more than anything else in their lives
- Being reckless and not caring about one's safety when using the drug
- Struggling financially since a lot of money is spent on purchasing the drug
- Neglecting relationships with others such as family members and friends

People who are struggling with Oxycodone dependence and addiction usually need to undergo a medical detoxification and continual treatment in order to get off the drug and prevent relapse.

Prolonged use of this drug, especially if not used as recommended by a medical doctor is considered as drug abuse. Individuals who take high doses of the drug either medically or recreationally may experience a wide array of effects, most of which are unpleasant. These include:

- Drowsiness
- Dizziness
- Euphoria
- Hallucinations
- Nausea
- Vomiting
- Reduced anxiety
- Calmness
- Relaxation
- Slowed breathing

Since the use of prescription opioids like Oxycodone is generally accepted in society, identifying and mitigating abuse and addiction can be quite challenging. In cases where users have prescriptions for the drug, it can be difficult to tell the difference between proper use and abuse. It generally boils down to the negative implications that the drug has on the life of the user. Nevertheless, one of the telltale signs of Oxycodone addiction is when a user's prescription typically runs out faster than the expected time. This can imply that the person is using more than the recommended dose of the drug.

It is worth noting that the use of Oxycodone can pose serious health risks to the individual. Like other opioids, Oxycodone usually causes depressed breathing, which may lead to severe medical issues such as unconsciousness, brain damage, and fatality. Even if you are using the drug prescriptively for pain relief, there are a number of safety precautions that you ought to follow. These include:

- Inform your doctor of any allergic reactions you may have to Oxycodone or any other ingredients in the medication you plan to take
- Make sure your doctor or pharmacist is aware of any other medications, vitamins or herbs that you are taking or planning to take concurrently with the Oxycodone medication
- Tell your doctor if you're breastfeeding
- Inform your doctor of any surgical procedures you may have undergone recently
- Do not use any heavy machinery or drive when taking this medication until you know how exactly the drug affects you
- Talk to your doctor about modifying your diet when taking Oxycodone in order to prevent constipation

Patients who are taking Oxycodone are often advised to have the drug Naloxone readily available. This drug is used to block the effects of opioids and reverse their symptoms. In the case of an opioid overdose, Naloxone is usually administered to patients in order to avert damage to the patient's organs and prevent fatality. Since you may not be able to treat yourself in the event of an overdose, you should ensure that your family members, caregivers or roommates know how to identify symptoms of an overdose and how to administer Naloxone in case of an overdose, before emergency services arrive.

Hydromorphone

Hydromorphone is an opioid derivative of morphine which is commonly given as a painkiller medication due to its analgesic properties. This drug is known to bind to different types of brain receptors including mu-opioid, kappa, and delta receptors. Hydromorphone is available in the form of oral tablets sold under brand names such as Exalgo which is an extended-release form and Dilaudid which is an immediate-release version. The onset of release of the immediate release version of hydromorphone is usually achieved in 15 to 20 minutes whereas the extended-release form of the drug may take up to 6 hours to become effective.

Apart from the oral pill forms of the drug, hydromorphone is also available in the form of an injectable solution and an oral liquid solution. This drug is usually prescribed for pain relief purposes in cases where other medications are ineffective. Hydromorphone is also sometimes used together with other medications in combined therapies.

Hydromorphone, like most opioid drugs, induces a wide variety of side effects. Some of the most common symptoms that may be experienced shortly after taking the drug include:

- Drowsiness
- Dizziness
- Insomnia
- Lightheadedness
- Sweating
- Euphoria
- Itching

These mild effects usually taper off or completely disappear after a few days or weeks. In some cases, more severe side effects can be experienced by patients who medicate using hydromorphone. Some of the more adverse side effects of this opioid drug include:

- Increased or slowed down heart rate
- Chest pains
- Vision problems such as blurry vision, double vision, and constricted pupils
- Abdominal discomfort
- Diarrhea
- Involuntary muscle movement
- Drastic changes in mood
- Psychological problems such as anxiety and depression
- Insomnia
- Breathing problems

In order to minimize the risk of adverse symptoms, hydromorphone is to be used in the right amounts.

HOW DO OPIOIDS WORK IN THE BRAIN?

One of the biggest misconceptions about opioid addiction is that individuals abuse these drugs simply to feel the euphoric effects that they are known to induce. Although this perception is not baseless, it does not fully capture the dynamics of opioid action in the brain that leads to addiction. While many individuals start taking opioids to manage pain, the drastic changes that occur in the brain as a result often lead to tolerance and dependency.

How *do* opioid drugs affect the brain?

Generally, opioids act on the brain by binding to the receptors that are responsible for how we perceive sensations such as pleasure and pain. Once an opioid drug such as heroin or codeine is ingested, the enzymes in the brain quickly convert it to morphine, which has pain-relieving properties. The process of binding usually causes large amounts of the hormone dopamine to be released, which is why users often feel euphoric upon taking prescription opioids. The problem with this is that the flood of dopamine in the brain may exceed what the body is normally capable of producing.

As an individual continues to take opioid drugs habitually, the brain begins to adapt to the increased levels of dopamine. Consequently, the body starts to develop a tolerance for the drug. When this happens, frequent opioid users find themselves in need of more drugs to feel normal. At this stage, they have become dependent and addicted to the drug, and their drug use is no longer a conscious decision.

Addiction is undoubtedly one of the serious effects of habitual opioid use on the brain, and can lead to serious mental health problems. Once addiction has taken hold, it can be very difficult for an individual to stop taking opioids due to withdrawal effects. This can significantly increase their drug use and put the victims in a vicious cycle, which could end in serious damage to one's health or even death.

Some of the habits and mental changes that may be brought about by long-term opioid use include:

- Poor memory/forgetfulness
- Inability to regulate one's actions
- Reduced flexibility when it comes to accomplishing tasks
- Diminished reasoning ability
- Poor decision-making skills
- Inability to plan

In most cases, the negative effects of prolonged opioid use are very difficult to reverse. These can take a serious toll on one's overall health and wellbeing, and can increase the risk of developing psychological problems such as anxiety and depression. Once an individual has developed an opioid addiction, it can be very difficult, albeit possible, for them to recover.

Patients who are suffering from addiction often require a multilayered treatment plan, which involves medication as well as counseling. They also need support, not only from their loved ones, but from society at large. With the right help and treatment, recovery from opioid addiction is very possible regardless of the duration of time one has been ailing for.

In conclusion, this chapter has been invaluable in providing an in-depth analysis of opioid drugs, how they are made, and the implications that they have on one's mental health. Some of the key takeaways from this chapter include the following:

- There are three main types of opioids, namely, naturally-occurring opiates, semi-synthetic opioids, and fully synthetic opioids
- All opioids work by binding to the brain's receptors, causing dopamine to be produced in very high amounts
- Opioids tend to induce various short term effects, which may include nausea, vomiting, abdominal pain and discomfort, respiratory distress and many more
- Prolonged use of opioids leads to increased tolerance and dependence, which consequently cause users to become addicted to these drugs
- Opioids use may affect a person's mood, speech and poor memory

- Opioids must be strictly used under the guidance of a qualified medical practitioner to lower the risk of overdose, which may cause serious brain damage or fatality

Given the high risks that opioids expose users to, it is absolutely important for dependency and addiction to be diagnosed early. This can significantly improve the chances of successful treatment, and may lower the risk of serious damage and death.

In the next chapter, we are going to look at some of the tell-tale signs of addiction, and how one can pick on them early before the problem spirals out of control. By doing so, an individual who is suffering from opioid addiction can be provided with the necessary assistance and rehabilitation to fully recover from these drugs.

4

SIGNS OF ADDICTION AND HOW TO NOTICE THEM EARLY

Opioids, like other drugs and medications, are essentially chemical in nature. This means they have the ability to alter our brain and body chemistry in fundamental ways. Notably, they not only have the power to alter how we feel, but also the way we think. It is inevitable, then, that an individual who is dependent on or addicted to these drugs will manifest certain signs and symptoms. Early diagnosis of these symptoms is absolutely important as it makes it possible for treatment to be administered before the condition gets out of hand.

Despite knowing the importance of early detection and treatment, the signs of opioid addiction aren't always very obvious. In cases where individuals are using prescription drugs to manage various kinds of pain, it can be difficult to tell whether the patients are addicted to the drugs or using them pragmatically to soothe their pain. In this chapter, we will cover some of the tell-tale signs of addiction, and how to pick up on them easily. We shall also look at factors that may predispose an individual to opioid addiction.

ADDICTION MODELS

Opioid tolerance, dependence, and addiction are all directly linked to the changes that the brain undergoes when introduced to opioid drugs. When an addict is trying to recover, they are fighting to reverse these changes.

In the early stages of opioid abuse, the stimulatory effects of these drugs on the mesolimbic reward system is what drives individuals to consume them. Once the inclination to use opioids continues to build up, however, users of these drugs may become dependent on them.

In general, the exposure of the brain to opioids interferes with the ability of the body to function optimally on its own. This exposure and interference continues its prompts to take the drugs to achieve the desired effects.

Over the years, various models have been proposed to describe the problem of addiction. Let us now briefly discuss some of these theories, and how they have influenced the understanding and treatment of drug addiction.

Automatic Processing Theories

These models of drug addiction are built around the assumption that addiction is shaped without the need for conscious intentions or decision making. In other words, Automatic Processing Theories explore ideas of addiction happening in the absence of our self-regulatory mechanisms. There are various theories that fall under the Automatic Processing model of drug addiction. They include:

- Learning Theories - These models hold that addiction stems from learning the relationships between responses, cues, and powerful reinforcers, which may be either positive or negative.

- Drive Theories - These link addiction to homeostatic processes such as cravings, which act as powerful motivating factors for drug use.
- Inhibition Dysfunction Theories - These models propose that addiction is the result of the impairment of regulatory mechanisms, which are meant to control our impulses with regard to drug use.
- Imitation Theories - These models link addiction to the inclination of individuals to imitate the actions of group members.

In response to these models of addiction, treatment is usually predicated on learning alternative practices, avoiding triggering stimuli for drug use, and increasing control of addictive habits. Under these models, treatment is more focused on developing new associations through training and repetition to overcome the problem of drug use. Medication may also be used to block actions that reinforce drug use and stimulate the process of change.

Reflective Choice Theories

These models are based on the assumption that human activities are, to some extent, influenced by a self-conscious evaluation of options and available alternatives. The main Reflective Choice Theories that are used to describe drug addiction are:

- Rational Choice Theory - This model holds that drug addiction is the result of rational choices made by an individual who believes that the benefits of using these addictive drugs far outweigh the cost of doing so.

- Biased Choice Theory - This model of addiction is based on the assumption that whereas an individual does make a reflective choice, they are subject to the effects of factors such as emotions, which may reduce the quality of choice made and even result in counterproductive decisions.

According to this perspective of drug addiction, treatment can be achieved by changing the benefit/cost ratio. This is done by increasing the cost of addictive habits and/or increasing the benefits of non-addictive actions to alter the individual's perception of this ratio.

Goal-Focused Theories

These models place greater emphasis on the goal of addictive practises. Some of the theories that support these models of drug addiction include:

- Positive Reward Theories - The model of Positive Rewards considers the pleasure and satisfaction that arises from drug use as the motivating factor for addiction. These rewards may be induced psychologically; for example, the euphoria that drug users experience when they take these substances. The rewards can also be more objective-based; for instance, taking drugs to alleviate chronic pain.
- Acquired Need Theories - In these models of addiction, the physiological rewards of taking addictive substances are thought to result in habituation and adaptation. The withdrawal effects that result from the habitual use of drugs, and the

strong aversion to those effects, is consequently seen as the driving force behind addiction.

- Identity and Identification Theories - These theories on addiction posit that addictive habits may be influenced by the presence of self-destructive or anti-social elements. So, a person who's intent on losing weight, for instance, may be driven to take up smoking as a means of achieving that objective.

From the standpoint of these Goal-Focused Theories, the problem of addiction stems from the desire of an individual to meet certain needs. Successful treatment aims at reducing the pleasure of addictive practices by enhancing one's internal control mechanism via medication. Another strategy involves counseling designed to help the user to find alternative sources of pleasure and personal fulfillment.

Integrative Theories

Integrative models of drug addiction are built on the premise that drug addiction stems from a complex interrelation of numerous factors, including the environment and the internal state of an individual. These factors interact with automatic or conscious processes targeting pleasure and avoiding physical or mental discomfort. The most common Integrative Theory on drug addiction is the Self-Regulation model. This theory is predicated on the ability of an individual to counteract their immediate reaction towards their desires and impulses. It assumes that a person's ability to counter these impulses may be limited by lack of skills, strategy, and capacity.

Other integrative theories approach the problem of addiction from an even wider scope. These models relate one's habits and traits with the environment and social context in which they exist. Consequently, they try to overcome the limitations of more specific models by integrating the various factors that influence drug addiction in a single unified model.

In light of the broad scope of Integrative models of addiction, treatments tend to make reference to some of the strategies that are commonly employed in more specific models. In this sense, Integrative Theories of substance addiction are generally more inclusive in their approach to treatment options

Biological Theories

In Biological models, addiction is considered to be a disease of the brain under the general assumption that the neural functioning of addicts is very different from that of non-addicts. Biological Theories also hold that various parameters influence the process of drug dependence and addiction including genetics, environmental factors, and physiological factors. Since human behavior is related to brain activity, all these factors are believed to give rise to addiction by acting on the neural processes of an individual's brain.

Under these models, treatment for addiction is focused on medications and therapies that are designed to change the way the brain of an addicted individual operates.

Process of Change Theories

While most models of addiction aim to describe how and why substance addiction develops, the Process of Change Theories mainly focus on how individuals recover. These models endeavor to optimize intervention strategies according to a general step-by-step model of change in an individual's habits and attitudes towards addictive substances. These interventions are usually adapted to the different stages of addiction in order to achieve maximum effect and avoid a relapse.

KNOWN RISK FACTORS OF OPIOID MISUSE AND ADDICTION

Opioid addiction usually happens when these prescription drugs are taken contrary to the recommendations of a physician; for instance, crushing a pill so that it can be snorted. This habit can be very dangerous and life-threatening especially if the drug has a lengthy action period. When the drug is rapidly delivered into the body, an overdose may occur. This can lead to serious damage to organs such as the brain, heart, liver, and may result in fatalities.

Studies have shown that the duration of time in which a person uses prescription opioids may raise the risk of addiction. Using these drugs for more than a few days, for instance, increases the likelihood of habitual use and addiction. There are various other factors that may significantly increase the risk of opioid addiction. These include:

Poverty and Unemployment

The relationship between poverty and drug addiction has been a subject of interest for many years. It is obviously very strange to think that individuals who have a low-income can afford the expensive lifestyle that comes with habitual drug use. Studies have shown, however, that poverty may contribute to drug addiction in a number of ways.

First, people of low socio-economic status are far more likely to abuse drugs than those who are wealthier. This is because when an economy is not thriving, individuals who have no job (and have more time on their hands) are more likely to use drugs. They are consequently at higher risk of becoming addicted than those who have full-time jobs.

Moreover, people who are addicted to drugs and live in poor conditions are less likely to be able to access treatment and rehabilitation centers. This means they are at risk of being hooked on drugs for longer.

Users living in poverty are also likely to get addicted to drugs, since they are more exposed to the drug trade, and may find the sale of drugs to be a lucrative activity. This may make it difficult for them to stay sober.

Family History of Substance Abuse

Studies have shown a correlation between family history and substance addiction. For instance, children who are raised by parents who habitually take drugs are at higher risk of addiction later in life. This is because they are likely to mimic the actions of their caregivers.

Personal History of Substance Abuse

Having a personal history of substance abuse can increase the risk of an individual becoming addicted to opioids. A person who has used drugs in the past may find it much easier to access them. This makes them more likely to become addicted to prescription opioids. Furthermore, individuals who are trying to quit opioids may easily relapse when not provided with the right treatment and support.

Age

Studies have shown that drug abuse and addiction are not limited to a particular age group. Younger individuals may be more inclined to take drugs recreationally due to peer pressure. On the other hand, studies have shown that older individuals (age 65+) who use opioid medications are at greater risk of dying from opioid overdose.

History of Criminal Activity or Legal Problems, Including DUIs

Criminal actions are closely associated with drug addiction. This is due to the fact that when most individuals commit crimes, they are usually under the influence of some kind of drug. For this reason, people who have a history of criminal activities are at greater risk of developing an addiction.

Regular Contact With High-Risk People or High-Risk Environments

Drug addiction is a prevalent problem in low-income neighborhoods where unemployment is rampant, and individuals often have to resort to selling drugs in order to survive. Those who are regularly exposed to high-risk persons such as drug dealers and users are at high risk of becoming addicts themselves.

Mental Disorders

Opioid addiction disorders are often associated with mental disorders. This is because people who suffer from mental illnesses like anxiety and depression are likely to use drugs in a bid to get rid of their pain. Conversely, symptoms of drug addiction are known to further exacerbate mental illnesses. As a result, many mentally ill people who also use opioids are at high risk of being stuck in a cycle of addiction.

Risk-Taking or Thrill-Seeking Actions

Individuals who habitually engage in risk-taking activities are more likely to become addicted to drugs than their more cautious counterparts. Drugs such as opioids tend to alter habits by causing changes in the brain. This can lower an individual's inhibition and make them daring and fearless. So, when people take drugs (*regularly*) in order to lower their inhibitions, they may end up becoming addicted to the thrill and become habitual users.

Stressful Circumstances

As human beings, we encounter challenging situations regularly in the course of our lives. Different people cope with stressful circumstances in their lives differently. While some may resort to confiding in their close friends and loved ones, others deal with stressful situations by indulging in opioid substances.

Career Path or Occupation

Research has shown that certain careers may increase the risk of drug use and addiction. For instance, in the arts and entertainment industry, there are a lot of famous actors, musicians, and other leading figures who have been in the news for illnesses or deaths due to drug use and abuse. This is not the only field that has such a high rate of addiction. Other career paths with the highest rates of drug and substance addiction include:

- Food and Hospitality Industry - According to reports by *Restaurant Business Online*, the food and hospitality industry has one of the highest rates of drug abuse, especially when it comes to illegal drugs. One in every five people working in this industry engages in the illicit use of drugs on a regular basis. In addition to taking illegal substances, employees also have a high rate of alcohol use as well as prescription opioids. The high prevalence of addiction is widely attributed to long working hours, and the pressure to perform at a very high level of customer service.

- Mining and Construction - The construction and mining industry is another career field that records very high numbers of drug abuse. According to the *Construction Executive Risk Management* magazine, 15 percent of construction workers regularly engage in the use of illicit drugs, while 18 percent frequently take alcohol. The high rate of drug and alcohol abuse in the construction industry often leads to serious injury, illnesses, and reduced productivity. Most of these employees hide their drug problems from their employers because they are afraid of losing their jobs. This usually exacerbates the problem and makes it even harder to mitigate.

- Business Management - The high-powered and fast-paced career of business management is known to be a great stress factor for professionals working in these fields. It is not surprising that a large number of business executives have been diagnosed with substance addiction. To deal with the stress experienced at the workplace, some managers often resort to the use of prescription opioids and other substances. This usually doesn't yield the desired results: Although the drugs provide temporary relief, the long term effects of prolonged use can be catastrophic. In light of this, numerous drug recovery programs now offer executive treatment plans that allow patients to continue working even as they undergo treatment. These programs also guarantee patients' privacy and confidentiality in order to ensure their professional lives are not negatively impacted.

- Healthcare Sector - It may seem ironic that the healthcare sector has a high prevalence of substance addiction, but many doctors and nurses are adversely affected by drug addiction. According to the National Council of State Boards of Nursing, career nurses who work in highly stressful situations are at high risk of drug use and abuse. Some of the nurses who are more susceptible to substance addiction include those working in tasking environments such as emergency rooms, oncology centers, and psychiatric wards. The high rate of drug use and abuse in the healthcare sector can be attributed to the ease of access to these drugs. Most medical practitioners work in environments where prescription drugs can be easily acquired.

SIGNS OF ADDICTION

Drug abuse and addiction typically affect people differently depending on the factors that we highlighted in the previous section. There are, however, various symptoms that are common to drug users. These common symptoms may provide important insights on whether an individual has an addiction problem. These include:

Physical Dependence

Prolonged use of both legal and illegal opioids often leads to a build-up of tolerance. When this happens, a person may not be able to feel normal when they use their usual doses of a drug. As we all are aware, the build-up of tolerance may lead to addiction problems. As a result, the affected person may get used to drugs to a point where they are unable to function normally without them.

Signs of Outward Harm

Addiction to opioids often takes a toll on one's physical and mental health, as well as their habits. That is why individuals who are addicted to these drugs may expose themselves to hazardous situations in order to get their quick fix. They are also likely to neglect their social roles as well as personal health.

Compulsion to Use

The compulsion to use drugs is one of the most common signs of opioid addiction. Individuals who have used these drugs for prolonged periods may find it difficult to refrain from using them. Moreover, due to their high tolerance, they may start using larger amounts in order to experience the same effects, and they may find themselves using drugs for longer amounts of time.

Reduced Tolerance for Pain

Prescription opioids, as we discussed in the previous chapters, are designed to provide relief for mild and chronic pain. Doctors often recommend them for pain management in patients who are experiencing post-surgery pain or terminal illnesses. However, when these drugs are abused, they can interfere with one's neurol system, and make them have a reduced tolerance for pain. Such individuals may end up being addicted to opioids as they use them habitually to get rid of the pain.

Impaired Cognition

Prolonged use of opioid drugs may interfere with cognitive function in a number of ways. For instance, they may affect the brain's white matter, which is responsible for decision-making and memory. Long-term opioid users may manifest an inability to make decisions and respond to threatening situations appropriately.

Other signs of opioid dependency and addiction include:

- Constricted pupils
- Confusion
- Depression
- Constipation
- Runny nose
- Coordination problems
- Poor awareness of one's environment

Apart from the general symptoms of opioid abuse, there are several withdrawal symptoms that can help identify whether an individual is suffering from addiction. These include:

- Anxiety
- Uncontrollable shaking
- Sweating
- Intense cravings
- Vomiting
- Insomnia
- Abdominal discomfort

Unlike addictive drugs like marijuana, opioids generally have a very high risk of overdose. People who habitually use opioids, especially illegal ones like fentanyl, have a very high chance of overdosing. This is due to the fact that these outlawed drugs are often manufactured in combination with other dangerous substances such as cocaine and metham-phetamines. It is not surprising, then, that most opioid-related overdoses are attributed to the use of illegal opioids.

An opioid overdose can cause serious damage to one's body organs, and may lead to death. In order to reverse the effects of the drug and to save lives, immediate treatment should be administered to opioid overdose patients. Here are some of the common signs and symptoms of opioid overdose:

- Constricted pupils
- Depressed breathing
- Drowsiness
- Confusion
- Drastic mood changes
- Uncontrolled vomiting
- Unconsciousness

In view of the life-threatening risks of opioid overdose, an individual who is suspected of having overdosed should be treated urgently to prevent fatality.

HOW OPIOID ADDICTION AFFECTS RELATIONSHIPS

Prolonged use of opioid drugs has the potential to completely alter an individual's temperament and actions. Consequently, this behavior can lead to social problems that deeply impact one's relationships in various ways, including:

Lies and Deception

One of the issues that people who are suffering from addiction struggle with is the need to maintain secrecy about their drug problem. This can be attributed to the stigma around drug addiction. Most opioid addicts are usually afraid of being judged by their friends, relatives, and society at large, due to their drug problem and they shame they may feel. They may also fear getting reported to authorities, losing their jobs or being victims of prejudice. As a result, they may go to extreme lengths to keep their habit a secret, and this may lead to turmoil in their relationships.

Loss of Trust

Due to their secretive lives and constant lying, people who

struggle with opioid addiction are likely to experience trust issues in their relationships.

Furthermore, an opioid addict may prioritize their drug habit more than their partners, families, and friends. This can erode trust and cause turmoil in their relationships. Once this happens, it can be very challenging for the drug user to rebuild trust without first undergoing treatment for their drug problem.

Domestic Violence and Abuse

The pent up frustration and resentment that comes with addiction can easily blow over and manifest in angry outbursts leading to serious implications. Individuals who are addicted to drugs tend to be highly irritable, especially when they are experiencing withdrawal effects. This makes them easily triggered by even the most minute problems. Under these circumstances, a simple altercation can easily turn into a violent rage, which may have fatal consequences. Close family members such as the spouses and children of opioid addicts are at more risk of being victimized by their addicted family members.

Enabling Relationships

Sometimes, having a relationship with an individual who suffers from a drug problem can cloud one's judgment, and make them complicit in abetting the problem. They may end up making choices that enable their loved one's drug habit, without even being aware of it. Some examples of enabling habits include:

- Taking up the responsibilities of an individual who is addicted to opioids when they are unable to perform them.

- Downplaying or minimizing the negative consequences of a loved one's drug problem.
- Accepting blame for a loved one's drug addiction.
- Availing drugs to an addicted individual when they experience withdrawal symptoms.
- Proving financial assistance to addicted individuals in order to fund their substance use and abuse.

It is very easy for an individual to miss the thin line between helping a struggling loved one and abetting their drug habit. This is why most people often end up exacerbating their loved one's addiction despite their best intentions. Often, these people act with good intentions without realizing that they are actually endangering the lives of addicted individuals.

Co-Dependent Relationships

Opioid addiction often results in co-dependent relationships, which are toxic to both parties. A codependent partner who is in a relationship with an opioid addict may be suffering from the consequences of their loved one's addiction, while at the same time, strongly holding a sense of duty towards them. They may feel that it is their responsibility to take care of their loved one and help them overcome their addiction. They may even enjoy serving in the role of caregiver to their loved ones.

While there is nothing inherently wrong about wanting to care for a drug addict, being too self-sacrificing can seriously affect one's physical and mental health, especially if the outcome expected is not forthcoming. Even though it's very noble to be concerned about a struggling loved one, take care not to be at the center of the addiction in their lives. In doing so, you will be able to remain grounded and rational even as you contend with the dynamic nature of the relationship with your addicted loved one.

As we come to the conclusion of the first half of this book, let us recap some of the most important takeaways from this chapter.

- Several models can be used to map the cause and progression of addiction. These include: Automatic Processing Theories; reflective Choice theories; Goal-Oriented Theories; and Integrative theories.
- An individual's risk of opioid addiction is influenced by a number of internal and external factors including poverty, unemployment, exposure to high-risk individuals and environments, previous history of substance abuse, mental illness and many others.
- Prolonged opioid use can significantly alter a person's habits and increase their risk of dependency and addiction. Consequently, this increases their chances of overdosing on these drugs, which can prove fatal.
- Opioid addiction can lead to loss of trust in relationships and increase the likelihood of domestic violence. This can significantly damage one's social life and contribute to further health problems such as depression.

At this point, I am certain that you now have a thorough understanding of the opioid problem, what causes addiction and the manner in which it presents in individuals. In the next and final half of this book, we are going to turn our attention to healing and discussing the strategies that can be applied to help an individual overcome opioid addiction. Some of the key topics that will be addressed in the coming chapters include: how to use prescription opioids safely and responsibly; how to incorporate medicines in the treatment of opioid addiction and the importance of seeking the help of others when fighting opioid addiction. Finally, we shall delve into non-drug and natural treatments that are available for preventing opioid addiction.

5

IF YOU NEED THEM, USE THEM RESPONSIBLY

Despite their addictive nature, there are moments when the use of opioid drugs may be necessary. For instance, if you are suffering from chronic pain due to injury, terminal illness or after surgery, your doctor may recommend an opioid medication to help manage the pain. If no other treatment is available, the use of prescription opioids might be the only viable option left. In light of the risks and dangers involved in opioid use, it is vital to take the necessary precautions to ensure that your health is not jeopardized. Having the right information about the effects of opioids, both positive and negative, can empower you to use these drugs responsibly if you require them for your pain-management needs.

Let us now turn our attention to some of the practices you need to cultivate in order to ensure you are using prescription opioids in the right manner. As you read this chapter, try to identify the key areas where you may need to improve when medicating with prescription opioids.

Stick to the Prescription

While prescription opioids are commonly prescribed to patients suffering from chronic pain, many individuals often fail to adhere to the instructions given by their doctors. Though many people tend to assume that failure to stick to the prescription is harmless, studies have shown that this practice can put one's health in serious jeopardy.

There are several reasons why many patients fail to adhere to the prescriptions instructions outlined by their physician. Some do so due to a lack of understanding of the directions given; some people fail to stick to the prescription due to forgetfulness. Individuals who are taking several medications at once are likely to forget the exact prescription of certain drugs. Unpleasant effects from the medication may also discourage an individual from using them in the right amounts. This is undoubtedly true with opioid medications, which are commonly known to produce serious side effects as we have discussed in the previous chapter.

The high cost of prescription opioids may also prevent some individuals from using the drugs as recommended. Patients who are unable to afford the drugs on a regular basis may opt to take fewer doses than what's prescribed to make the prescription last longer.

Regardless of one's motive for not adhering to the recommended prescription, not following directions can be very harmful and detrimental to one's health. Failure to stick to the required doses may cause the treatment to stall, and make the drug ineffective. This could cause the patient's condition to deteriorate so rapidly that they may end up being hospitalized. In more extreme cases, failure to take the right dosage may lead to fatality.

In light of these risks, sticking to the recommended prescription is very important especially when taking opioid medications. How can you ensure that you are following the regimen outlined by your doctor? Here are some of tips that can help you stick to your prescription:

- Schedule a specific time for taking your medication every day.
- Combine the time you take your medication with another activity such as preparing for bedtime, brushing your teeth, etc.
- Keep track of your medication using a 'calendar.' Make sure you keep a record of the pills you take on a daily basis.
- When traveling, make sure you bring enough pills to last several extra days in case your return is delayed.
- Use a pill container to organize the drugs according to the time of day that you are supposed to take them, e.g., breakfast, lunch, after dinner, etc.

Make Sure You Know the Risks

Before starting any prescription opioid regimen, it is essential to be informed of the risk factors involved. Whereas opioid drugs are very effective when it comes to pain management, there are numerous risks that they may pose to the patients who take them. Apart from the negative side effects that we highlighted in the previous chapters, some of these drugs have interactions with other medications, herbs, and food, which may result in morbidity and mortality.

The interaction of prescription opioids with other drugs can be classified as either pharmacodynamic or pharmacokinetic. The former refers to interactions in which the drugs influence each other's effects directly. In such a case, when the two drugs are administered concurrently, the concentration-response of one or both of the drugs is altered without any change in the pharmacokinetics of the object drug.

Pharmacodynamic drug-drug interactions can be either additive, synergistic or antagonistic. An additive interaction is a situation whereby the effect of the two substances is equal to the sum of the effect of the two drugs taken separately, whereas in a synergistic interaction the effect of two drugs when used together is greater than the sum of their separate effect at the same doses. Conversely, an antagonistic interaction is a situation where the effect of two drugs is less than the sum of the effect of the two drugs when taken separately.

On the other hand, a pharmacokinetic drug-drug interaction happens when one drug (a precipitant) interferes in the absorption, distribution, metabolism, and excretion of the other drug (the object). This type of interaction can lead to a reduction in the concentration of an opioid drug, thereby making it less therapeutic and effective.

The interaction of prescription opioids with other medications may also have adverse effects on persons with pre-existing medical conditions. The pharmacodynamic interactions of opioids may, for instance, increase the risk of respiratory depression in patients who have cardiovascular or cerebrovascular conditions. Patients who have brain injuries, dementia or psychiatric illnesses are also at higher risk of cognitive impairment when exposed to opioid medications.

Likewise, individuals who have a history of substance abuse are more likely to develop dependence and addiction to prescription opioids compared with those who have never used drugs.

Questions to Ask your Doctor

In order to use prescription opioids responsibly, it is essential to be sufficiently informed about these drugs. If you intend to use these drugs to manage your medical condition, there are several questions you may ask your doctor in order to receive clarification on their suitability to your condition. These questions include:

i) Why was I prescribed opioids and are they the best option for me?

You may be well aware by now that prescription opioids are generally used as pain-relief medications. Doctors often recommend these drugs to patients who are suffering from chronic pain due to physical injury, terminal illness, and recent surgery. If you are experiencing pain due to any of these reasons, there is a chance that your doctor may prescribe an opioid drug to help you cope with the pain.

Since these drugs often come with a whole slew of side effects, you should make sure you understand these possible side effects that you may have to deal with when medicating on opioids. If you are in chronic pain, prescription opioids may be the only option you have despite the unpleasant side effects that may accompany their use. On the other hand, if your pain is mild, there are various non-drug options that may be more appropriate and safer to use.

Before you start taking these drugs, your doctor should explain why they are prescribing them, and they should offer alternatives in case the drugs fail to deliver desired results, based on your situation.

ii) Will opioids cause side-effects that could affect the quality of my life?

Prescription opioids are very powerful and potent drugs that produce a wide array of side effects. Apart from the physical effects such as respiratory distress, sweating, vomiting, and abdominal pains, opioid use may also cause long-lasting cognitive changes. Individuals who use these drugs for prolonged periods of time may experience significant mood changes, increased tolerance, dependence, and possible addiction. All of these effects have serious implications on a user's overall health and wellbeing.

Before starting out on prescription opioids, it is important to be aware of both the short-term and long-term effects that these drugs may have on your health.

iii) Should I be concerned about starting opioids/stopping them?

Prolonged use of opioid medications is known to cause tolerance build-up, which may lead to dependency. Even individuals who use these drugs as prescribed by a doctor may end up developing a high tolerance for them. This can reduce the effectiveness of the medication and necessitate an increase in dosage. As a result, people who regularly use these drugs may end up becoming hooked on them. This is obviously a serious concern to take into account when making the decision on whether or not to use these drugs.

In cases where addiction has set in, it may be very difficult to abstain from prescription opioids due to the withdrawal symptoms that they are likely to experience. Furthermore, the long-term use of prescription opioids for pain management can significantly reduce one's tolerance for pain. As a result, an individual may end up using the drugs perpetually.

iv) What are other pain management treatments?

The fact that you may be experiencing chronic pain does not automatically mean that prescription opioids are the solution. Whereas these drugs can be highly effective in providing pain relief, they also come with a lot of unpleasant side-effects, which might be more detrimental to your health. If possible, try to explore other treatment methods that may be more suitable for your condition before deciding whether or not to use opioids.

There are various non-pharmacological therapies that can be used to manage chronic pain. These include treatments such as acupuncture, relaxation techniques, massage therapy, and gel packs. Being aware of the various non-drug therapies available can help you make the right choice when deciding on the safest pain management treatment to apply.

v) Could a physician who specializes in pain management help me?

Having a specialized therapist can be invaluable when it comes to chronic pain management. A qualified specialist can evaluate your condition and devise the right treatment strategy for your situation. Depending on your health status, they may recommend using opioids, non-drug treatments or a combination of both.

Keep them Out of the Reach of the People Living around You.

One of the factors that contribute to the misuse and abuse of prescription drugs is the practice of sharing. Many individuals who have prescriptions of these drugs often feel inclined to share with their friends or relatives. This practice can have serious implications for all individuals involved, due to a number of reasons.

Sharing your prescription opioids with others reduces your consignment, and may shorten your dosage. This can force you to cut down on the recommended prescription. Consequently, this can jeopardize the effectiveness of the medication and cause the entire treatment to fail.

The practice can also put your close relatives and friends at serious risk. As we have reiterated several times over the course of this book, opioids are very potent drugs that must be consumed under the recommendations of a qualified medical professional. By using these drugs without a prescription, an individual risks developing tolerance, dependence and addiction, which can be very difficult to treat.

For this reason, it is important to ensure that you use the drugs responsibly. Do not share them with anyone, and always store your drugs safely to prevent them from falling into the wrong hands, e.g. young children.

Know When It's Time to Stop

One of the hardest things about using prescription opioids is knowing when it is time to stop using them, and how to make that transition. Opioids are naturally addictive, partly due to the pleasant symptoms they induce. In addition to their pain-relieving properties, prescription opioids often generate feelings of sedation and euphoria when ingested. That's why when an individual becomes too accustomed to this feeling, it may be very difficult for them to quit using these drugs, even when the original purpose of using them has already been achieved.

In order to use these drugs responsibly, you need to realize when the drugs have served their purpose, and you no longer need them. Your physician or anesthesiologist can help you come off these drugs by doing the following:

- Individualizing your tapering plan to minimize the effects of your withdrawal symptoms
- Constantly monitoring your withdrawal effects
- Adjusting the rate and duration of your tapering process appropriately, depending on the withdrawal effects that you are experiencing
- Recommending additional sources of support that can help you give up the drugs safely

Watch out for Withdrawal Symptoms

When opioids are used for extended periods of time, they may lead to a condition known as opioid withdrawal syndrome. This arises out of drug dependency, and is characterized by the inability of an individual to function normally without using the opioids. The rate at which individuals develop dependency varies from person to person. Once they have become dependent on these drugs, it can be very difficult for them to function without taking them.

If you are trying to quit using opioids, you need to realize that it will take some time for the body to shed off its addiction to the drugs and begin functioning normally again. That's why it is crucial to pay close attention to the symptoms that are manifesting, as you cut down on and eventually quit opioid use.

Some of the early stage withdrawal symptoms that you need to keep an eye on include:

- Insomnia
- Muscle aches and pains
- Sweating
- Nausea
- Vomiting

- Diarrhea

In addition to these short-term symptoms, there are several long-term withdrawal symptoms that you may experience when you first try to quit opioid use. These include:

- Abdominal cramping
- Increased heart rate
- Uncontrollable shaking
- Dilated pupils

Although these withdrawal symptoms are not life-threatening, they can be very uncomfortable and painful to endure when you are trying to give up on opioid use. These symptoms are key indicators of how your body is coping with the absence of opioids. By observing these symptoms, your anesthesiologist can be able to determine the right dose for you at every stage, during the process of giving up on opioids.

TRY SEEKING ALTERNATIVE PAIN RELIEF PRACTICES

Dealing with constant chronic pain can be challenging for anyone. Most people end up seeking prescription opioids for their pain-relieving properties. There are, though, several alternative treatments that can be used to alleviate chronic pain. These non-drug options are not only effective, but also desirable, since they do not produce adverse side effects that are commonly associated with prescription opioids. Some of the alternative non-pharmacological treatments that you can opt for include:

Combined Therapy

In most cases, opioids by themselves are not very useful

when it comes to pain management; they may cause negative side effects which may jeopardize the treatment. As a result, many physicians often recommend combined therapy involving both the use of opioids and non-drug treatments to manage chronic pain. Since minimal amounts of opioids are used in combined therapy, the risk of developing tolerance and dependence is significantly low.

Non-Drug Therapies

In cases where opioids are ineffective or counterproductive to managing pain, patients can find relief with the help of non-drug therapies. Some of the most common non-drug treatments that may be recommended include acupuncture, meditation, biofeedback, and massage therapy. These treatments are very safe, and can be applied with little to no adverse side effects. If you are struggling with chronic pain, it is vital to seek help from an expert who will recommend the best non-drug therapy for you.

Injections or Implants

In case you are experiencing neuropathic pain or muscle spasms, getting a local anesthetic injection may be a sufficient alternative to short-circuit the pain. Similarly, if you are suffering from chronic pain in your arms, back, and legs, your physician may recommend getting a spinal cord stimulation procedure. This typically involves having a device implanted in a patient's back to block pain by transmitting electric pulses to the spinal cord and nerves. These alternative treatments can help you manage chronic pain much more effectively while protecting you from the numerous risks that are involved in pharmacological therapies.

The responsible use of opioid drugs is essential when it comes to pain-management therapy using these drugs.

Failure to observe the recommended precautions can put one at risk of significant physical and mental health problems. Here are the main takeaways on the practices that you should always uphold when using prescription opioids to relieve pain:

- Always use the medication in the right doses.
- Ensure that you are well informed on the risks that are involved with opioid use before you start using these drugs.
- Refrain from sharing your prescription opioids with your friends and family members.
- Always ensure that your drugs are stored safely away from the reach of children and other susceptible individuals.
- Look out for any withdrawal symptoms that you may be experiencing as you try to cut down or completely stop taking these drugs. Make sure to inform your doctor about these so that they can recommend the appropriate treatment for your condition.
- Seek non-drug therapies to help you manage your pain safely.

6

MEDICATION AS TREATMENT

While prescription opioids are very useful as pain-relief medication, the personal price of using them may at times be too high to bear. Once an individual starts using opioid drugs, their tolerance often builds up gradually until they are unable to operate normally without consuming high doses of the drug.

Persons that have used prescription opioids for long periods of time are likely to be stuck in a cycle of addiction unless they receive the right treatment and support. The treatment for addiction typically includes short term therapy to manage withdrawal symptoms, long-term treatment of withdrawal symptoms, and overdose treatment. The type of treatment administered often depends on the severity of the problem.

SHORT-TERM TREATMENT OF WITHDRAWAL SYMPTOMS

Opioid dependence is usually accompanied by withdrawal symptoms that range from mild to severe. Treatment for these symptoms is generally determined by their severity and duration. In general, the withdrawal symptoms of most opioids usually kick in 6 to 12 hours after use, and may last for up to 5 days. While these symptoms are not life-threatening, they can be very unpleasant. That is why individuals who are suffering from withdrawal symptoms are likely to relapse back to active drug use.

To break the cycle of addiction, it is essential for victims of opioid use disorder to receive immediate treatment. There are various indicators that influence the onset and duration of opioid effects. These include:

- If the drug is used intermittently, withdrawal effects are unlikely to appear
- High intake of prescription opioids for longer durations of time raises the risk of withdrawal effects
- Short-acting opioids and slowly injected morphine have a more rapid onset and shorter withdrawal duration
- Longer-acting opioids such as methadone have a slower onset but more lasting withdrawal symptoms

Medications such as buprenorphine and methadone have been approved by the FDA for short term treatment of opioid withdrawal symptoms. These drugs must be administered under the guidance of a qualified medical practitioner or physician.

LONG-TERM MAINTENANCE TREATMENT

Opioid dependence and addiction are highly complex health conditions that require long-term treatment and management. Early treatment can help an individual regain their physical and psychological health, thus enabling them to become functional and productive members of society.

The aim of long-term maintenance treatment is to successfully rehabilitate individuals who are struggling with opioid addiction, reduce their dependence on these drugs, and eliminate the risk of overdose. Since no single treatment is effective for treating all individuals who suffer from opioid addiction, therapy usually combines several treatments, including medication and behavioral therapy.

The FDA has approved various medications for opioid addiction treatment. These include the mu-opioid agonists methadone and buprenorphine or the opioid antagonist, naltrexone. Let us briefly discuss some of these pharmacological agents and how they work in relation to opioid addiction treatment.

Naltrexone

Naltrexone is an opioid antagonist drug that is commonly used to treat patients who suffer from addiction to opiate drugs like morphine, codeine, and heroin. The drug can also be used to treat individuals who are addicted to alcohol and recovering addicts to prevent a relapse.

Naltrexone generally works by blocking the effects of opioid drugs such as euphoria, pain relief, and sedation. Since most people tend to get hooked on opioids to experience these effects, the use of naltrexone treats addiction by eliminating the need or desire to use opioids.

This drug is typically administered orally, and can be consumed with or without food. It is also important for this treatment to be supervised by a professional physician so that they can keep track of the progress and note any effects that may be manifesting (in the early stages) in the patient.

Not all people, however, are allowed to take this drug. You are advised to avoid naltrexone if:

- You are still using other prescription opioids such as morphine, heroin, and methadone
- You experience extreme allergic reactions after taking the drug
- You are experiencing withdrawal symptoms from using other drugs or alcohol
- You have used any other opioid medication in the past 10 days

In order to ensure the safe use of this drug, you should inform your doctor if you have the following conditions:

- Liver disease
- Kidney disease
- Blood clot
- Respiratory illnesses

Using opioid medications while on naltrexone may induce withdrawal symptoms. Some of the most common side effects of using this drug include:

- Nausea and vomiting
- Diarrhea
- Mood changes
- Hallucination

- Confusion
- Depression
- Dizziness
- Insomnia

These symptoms are not life-threatening, and may taper off after a few days. If you do experience adverse effects, you should inform your doctor immediately. You should also refrain from sharing this medicine with others and store it safely away from the reach of children.

Buprenorphine

Buprenorphine is a weak partial mu-opioid receptor agonist used as an alternative medication for treating severe opioid addiction. It usually helps in fighting addiction by preventing the withdrawal symptoms resulting from halting the use of opioids. The drug is often used in combination with counseling sessions to provide a holistic treatment for opioid addiction.

Buprenorphine is usually administered orally - put it under the tongue and allow it to dissolve completely. It is often administered together with Naloxone to prevent misuse of the medication. For best results, buprenorphine should be given to a patient as soon as the first signs of withdrawal take effect. If the drug is administered soon after one has taken other opioid medications, withdrawal effects may ensue.

If one stops taking buprenorphine sooner than required, one may also experience adverse withdrawal effects including nausea, runny nose, diarrhea, and insomnia. For this reason, doctors are usually advised to slowly lower the dose administered to patients in order to prevent these symptoms.

Methadone

Methadone is an opioid drug that is used to relieve chronic pain in patients who need medication for pain management but cannot be treated by other drugs. This medication is also commonly used to prevent withdrawal symptoms in patients who are trying to recover from opioid addiction.

The drug works by blocking the effects of opioid medications such as heroin, codeine, and hydrocodone. Since it produces similar effects to other prescription opioids, methadone is commonly used as part of replacement therapy. It can also be combined with counseling and non-pharmacological therapies to maximize the effectiveness of the treatment.

Methadone comes in a variety of forms including tablets, powder, and liquid solutions. Although the drug is legal, and widely available in most pharmacies, one needs a doctor's prescription to obtain it. In most cases of opioid addiction, doctors recommend that methadone is used for at least a year during the recovery period. Once it is time to stop using the drug, your doctor will slowly reduce your dose of the drug to prevent withdrawal symptoms.

Some of the common side effects associated with this drug include:

- Restlessness
- Vomiting
- Respiratory depression
- Itchy skin
- Loss of appetite
- Abdominal discomfort
- Headache
- Mood changes

These symptoms are typically mild, and tend to dissipate after a few days. In some cases, severe symptoms may be experienced by individuals who are using methadone to treat opioid addiction. Some of the adverse side effects of using this drug may include:

- Fainting
- Swollen lips, tongue or face
- Faster heartbeat
- Seizures
- Drowsiness
- Trouble swallowing

LAAM (levomethadyl acetate)

LAAM is a synthetic opioid drug that works in a manner similar to methadone. This medication is usually administered to opioid-dependent individuals to block the effects of other opioid medications, thereby eliminating the craving for these drugs.

Just like methadone, LAAM has been approved by the FDA for treating opioid addiction. The effects of this drug are usually longer lasting compared to methadone. This makes it possible for LAAM to be taken on alternate days, unlike methadone which must be taken daily.

Like most opioid agonists, LAAM can cause physical dependence when used for prolonged periods. As a result, doctors often reduce the dosage gradually to prevent withdrawal symptoms from manifesting.

Some of the common side effects that are associated with this drug include:

- Muscle and joint pain

- Insomnia
- Constipation
- Nervousness
- Drowsiness
- Dizziness
- Poor concentration

LAAM should not be taken by patients who are using other prescription opioids, alcohol, benzodiazepines, and antidepressants. The drug is also not recommended for use during pregnancy as it can have adverse effects on the developing fetus.

Naloxone

Naloxone is an opioid antagonist drug that is used to block or reverse the effects of opioid medications including loss of consciousness, drowsiness, and slow breathing. This drug is commonly administered as an injection, especially in case of emergencies such as opioid overdose. Similarly, naloxone is used to diagnose whether an individual has overdosed on opioids.

There are various scenarios where the use of this drug is not recommended. These include:

- Pregnancy
- If one is taking alcohol or any other opioid drug
- If the individual is allergic to the drug
- If one is suffering from chronic conditions such as heart disease, liver disease, and respiratory illnesses
- If one is breastfeeding

Since naloxone works by reversing the effects of opioid medications, withdrawal symptoms may be experienced by persons using this drug. Some of the common side effects of this antagonist opioid include:

- Diarrhea
- Nausea and vomiting
- Stomach pain
- Fever
- Body aches
- Nervousness
- Irritability
- Runny nose

Naloxone is known to interact with other prescription and over-the-counter drugs, vitamins, and herbal products. Nevertheless, the drug is often used to treat opioid-related drug overdoses where it is administered as an emergency treatment. In such a scenario, it may not be possible to inform your doctor about your medical history, so the chances of developing complications are very high.

For this reason, if you are a friend or relative of the drug addict, it is important to provide any relevant information on the history of the patient that would help medical professionals to facilitate the recovery process.

TREATMENT OF OVERDOSE

People who use opioid medications either medically or recreationally are at very high risk of overdosing on these drugs. This risk is particularly greater for individuals who use illicit synthetic opioids like fentanyl. The overdose can lead to slowed breathing that can cause significant brain damage, organ failure, and even death. In light of this, immediate care should be administered to an overdose victim to save their lives, and prevent serious damage to their health.

Opioid overdose happens when an individual has excessive stimulation of the opiate pathway. This can cause respiratory depression and possibly lead to death. Some of the common causes of opioid overdose include:

- Therapeutic drug error
- Intentional overdose
- Unintentional overdose
- Complications related to opioid abuse

Possible signs and symptoms of an opioid overdose include:

- Slow /difficulty in breathing
- Unconsciousness
- Unresponsiveness to outside stimulus
- Vomiting
- Pale face and body
- Slow heartbeat
- Choking sounds

Initial treatment for an opioid overdose is usually administered depending on the vital signs. For instance, if a patient is comatose due to opioid overdose and is not breathing, they should first be provided with airway control before any further treatment is administered. An endotracheal intubation is often conducted to protect their airways. Thereafter, naloxone may be administered to reverse the effects of respiratory depression. It should be noted, however, that naloxone can also cause aggression or agitation, and must be administered in minimal amounts depending on a patient's response.

Once a patient has been provided with the first line of treatment at the scene of the overdose, they should be transferred to the emergency department of a hospital. If the patient has already received treatment for respiratory distress, the doctors should check for any signs of occult trauma to the cervical spine. In some cases, when patients who are suspected of having overdosed on opioids are transferred to the emergency room, they may have their blood glucose levels drawn.

Emergency treatment typically begins with supportive care, including respiratory assistance through CPR and removal of the opioid agent in the case of the drug having been delivered using a patch. If the doctor suspects an opioid overdose, the antagonist drug naloxone should be administered immediately either intravenously, subcutaneously or intramuscularly.

When administered intravenously, naloxone takes effect after a few minutes. A second dose may be given after 2 to 3 minutes. When naloxone is administered intramuscularly or subcutaneously, the onset action may take up to 10 minutes. Once the overdosed patient is awake, the dose of naloxone should be disconnected. In patients who overdose on opioids such as methadone and heroin, larger doses of naloxone should be administered.

Sometimes, naloxone is used in combination with buprenorphine to treat opioid overdose. The advantage of this drug combination is that it can reduce withdrawal symptoms for up to 36 hours.

Most patients who overdose on opioids and are treated with naloxone may be admitted to an emergency facility for monitoring for about 12 to 36 hours. Likewise, patients who require more than one dose of naloxone to reverse their overdose are also admitted for observation. Due to the risk of respiratory depression in emergency overdoses, many doctors are increasingly promoting take-home naloxone for high-risk opioid users.

Once a patient has been treated successfully for an opioid overdose, they should continually be provided with psychological counseling and therapy to help them overcome their opioid use, and avoid a relapse.

Although opioid addiction and overdose can be very destructive and life-threatening, it is possible for an individual to be treated successfully as long as they are diagnosed early and provided with immediate medical assistance.

As we come to the end of this chapter, here are the most important points to remember:

- There are several drugs that have been approved for opioid addiction treatment by the FDA. These include buprenorphine, naloxone, naltrexone, methadone and levomethadyl acetate (LAAM)
- Opioid antagonists should be administered to patients immediately to reverse the effects of opioid drugs and ease respiratory distress
- Individuals who are recovering from opioid addiction should reduce their dose of antagonist drugs gradually in order to reduce withdrawal effects.
- Opioid overdose patients may be hospitalized or treated outpatient depending on the severity of their symptoms once emergency care has been administered.

7

SEEK THE HELP OF OTHERS

In our society, there is a widely held perception that addiction is a personal problem that arises out of weakness of character or from making poor life choices. The idea that substance addiction is an actual illness that affects the physical and psychological balance of a person is still inconceivable to many people. As a result of this common misconception, many people tend to treat individuals who are struggling with addiction as outcasts who should be isolated from others lest they influence them negatively. This kind of response to addiction, however, usually does more harm than good. It is vital that we remind ourselves that those who suffer from addiction are human beings who deserve the care and protection of society just like everyone else. It is especially important that they are supported so that they can recover fully from addiction and become productive members of society.

In this section, we will highlight the role that family members, friends, and society all play in the fight against opioid addiction. If you are struggling with addiction yourself, this chapter will show you the importance of seeking the help of others to aid your recovery and the ways in which you can do that.

Clinical Psychology of Addiction

While opioid addiction is commonly regarded as a physical illness due to the physical symptoms that it manifests, this problem is also psychological to a great extent. Early on, we discussed the cognitive ramifications of addiction, and saw how the problem of opioid dependence and addiction can alter one's mood and cause an imbalance in mental states. Nevertheless, the disease of opioid addiction can also be triggered by several psychological issues. In order for the right treatment to be administered, it is important to understand the psychological aspect of addiction.

Although opioid addiction is mainly a result of various modifications in a person's body, recovery necessitates that those who are affected by this problem apply significant changes in their relationship with these drugs. Like most human actions, opioid addiction is a habit that is learned. Since psychology is the study of human practices, exploring the psychological makeup of opioid addicts can provide us with important insights into this condition and subsequently guide the decision toward the right approach to treatment.

Another psychological factor that may cause or perpetuate the problem of addiction is people's beliefs and thoughts. It is no secret that our own actions tend to be influenced by our thoughts and beliefs. This means an individual's beliefs about opioid addiction may determine whether or not they are able to overcome this disease. For instance, a person who believes they can't recover from opioid addiction is unlikely to put in the effort required to kick the habit. On the contrary, an individual who considers opioid addiction as a disease that can be treated is likely to be motivated to follow through on treatment, and exert themselves fully in trying to overcome this challenge.

Likewise, a person's level of developmental maturity may also influence whether or not they are able to overcome the problem of addiction. If an individual routinely acts according to every craving, desire or whim without exercising critical thinking, they are likely to become addicted to opioids due to low developmental maturity. The person may end up getting hooked on drugs simply because they act out of impulse without thinking about the ramifications of their actions.

Individuals who manifest opioid addiction as a result of these psychological comorbidities can be helped to overcome this disease through psychotherapy.

Drug Addiction and Mental Health Diagnosis

Numerous studies conducted over the past couple of years have established a link between drug addiction and mental health. It is estimated that at least 8.2 million adults who were suffering from addiction had concurrent mental illness diagnoses. Even more surprising is the fact that only 48 percent of these people received treatment for either their drug problem or mental illness. This means more than half of these respondents did not receive treatment for either of these conditions.

This shortage of treatment for dual diagnoses of addiction and mental illness can be attributed to the fact that very few rehabilitation programs are equipped to deal with these cases. As a result, most people who seek therapy for their opioid addiction and mental illnesses are not able to receive the treatment they require. This is undoubtedly a very unfortunate situation, considering the fact that individuals with concurrent disorders are at greater risk of relapsing.

Comprehensive treatment and care can significantly reduce the risk of relapse in individuals who are recovering from opioid addiction. In order for this to happen, there has to be a paradigm shift in which the problem of addiction is treated as a mental illness instead of a criminal activity or irresponsible behavior.

Opioid addiction is characterized as a mental illness because it causes significant changes in the brain, which can alter one's mood and actions in extreme ways. Once an individual becomes dependent on these substances, their ability to control their impulses and cravings is compromised. Consequently, an opioid addict may find it difficult to stop using these substances, even when they are aware of the dangers that they expose themselves to. This compulsive behavior is quite similar to the manner in which mentally ill individuals act.

How exactly should the treatment of addiction be approached when dealing with individuals who are also diagnosed with mental illness? Studies have shown that among patients with moderate to severe dual diagnoses disorders, the chances for successful treatment are higher when the addiction treatment is supplemented with targeted psychological therapies. Like most other mental health illnesses, opioid addiction often requires long-term treatment and maintenance. This is contrary to the commonly held belief that only will power is required in order to kick a drug habit.

The connection between mental health and drug abuse is not always as clear-cut as some may be inclined to think. Whereas opioid addiction can give rise to mental health problems, there are certain scenarios where the addiction problem itself arises out of poor mechanisms of coping with mental illness. For instance, some individuals may use drugs like morphine and heroin as a means of self-medicating their mental illnesses such as depression and anxiety. These strategies, however, often lead to catastrophic outcomes and may exacerbate the problem.

There are several ways in which the symptoms of mental illness and opioid addiction can trigger each other. These include:

- Chronic use of opioids can increase an individual's risk of being a victim of violent crime or rape, which may lead to mental health problems like PTSD and depression.
- Bad decisions made under the influence of opioid drugs can make one susceptible to criminal activities, which may get them in trouble and contribute to anxiety.

When it comes to dual diagnosis disorders, the treatment approach should encompass both addiction treatment as well as mental health therapies. Without a comprehensive treatment plan for dual diagnosis, the risk of patients relapsing to drug use is very high. If one's mental health symptoms are not fully treated, it can be very difficult for a person to remain sober and possibly provide an incentive for them to use opioids to self-medicate. Conversely, if their opioid addiction symptoms are not addressed through a comprehensive treatment model, the individual can spiral deeper into addiction, and consequently develop more serious mental health conditions.

DIFFERENT TREATMENT APPROACHES FOR DRUG ADDICTION

Although addiction is a treatable condition, it is also a very chronic problem that requires a multi-layered approach. Individuals who have developed a dependency on drugs cannot simply quit using drugs for a few days and be completely cured. Most patients of opioid addiction typically require long-term treatment and care in order to successfully overcome the habit. That is why treatment for opioid addiction should be focussed on helping individuals to stop using drugs in the short-term, become drug-free for the long-term, and return to being productive members of society.

There are various principles that should form the foundation of any addiction treatment. These include acknowledging that:

- Addiction is a complex disease, with the potential of completely altering a person's way of life.
- No single kind of treatment is suitable for everyone.
- Individuals who are struggling with addiction need to be able to access treatment quickly.
- In order for treatment to be effective, it needs to address all the patient's needs, not just their drug use.
- Counseling and behavioral therapies are essential in order for treatment to be effective.
- Medication is an integral part of opioid dependence and addiction treatment.
- Treatment programs should be reviewed regularly and customized to suit the ever-changing needs of the patient.

- Opioid addiction treatment should also address the mental health of the patient.
- The patients' drug use should be monitored constantly throughout the duration of treatment.
- Treatment need not be voluntary.

There are various treatment approaches that can be used to treat opioid addiction successfully. These include:

Cognitive-Behavioral Therapy (CBT)

This is a form of mental health counseling that is widely used in addiction treatment today. This psychological counseling is designed to help addicts find connections between their thoughts, emotions, and actions. This counseling increases their awareness of themselves and allows them to foster positive habits to overcome dependence.

In addition to treating addiction, CBT can be very effective when it comes to managing various mental illnesses including, bipolar disorder, obsessive-compulsive disorder, depression, and post-traumatic stress disorder.

How exactly does this therapy work? The goal of CBT is to help patients become more aware that not all of their thoughts, feelings, and actions are rational or logical. Through CBT, individuals who struggle with opioid addiction are able to develop a wider perspective on their illness and see the way in which past experiences and environmental factors influence their drug problem.

Cognitive-behavioral therapists assist individuals who are recovering from addiction to identify negative automatic thoughts that make them susceptible to opioid use. By continually revisiting painful thoughts and memories which they harbor within them, recovering addicts are able to reduce the pain caused by these painful thoughts and memories. The result is help to eliminate urges and impulses that may predispose them to opioid use. They are also able to learn positive practices, which can replace their addictive tendencies.

CBT allows opioid-dependent individuals to kick their addiction by:

- Helping overcome negative thoughts and beliefs which make them likely to use drugs.
- Training on how to communicate better with their friends and colleagues.
- Providing self-help techniques and tools which can help to improve their mood.

The therapy also trains opioid-dependent individuals to become aware of triggers that spark opioid cravings. Some of the skills that CBT aims to teach opioid-dependent individuals include:

- Recognition - This is the ability to identify the circumstances or situations that trigger the urge to use drugs. Being able to pick on the situations that make you susceptible to drug use is necessary in order to remove you from the triggering situations or handle it more positively.
- Avoidance - Patients are trained on how to remove themselves from situations that trigger the impulse to take opioid drugs.
- Coping - CBT provides patients with techniques and tools that can address the underlying thoughts and emotions, which often lead to drug abuse.

CBT can be administered in a therapist's office, remotely at home, in the form of individual therapy sessions or group therapy meetings where recovering opioid addicts can interact with and share their stories with others.

Twelve-Step Approaches

This treatment approach involves group meetings where individuals who are struggling with addiction can share their experiences with each other and find solidarity, comfort, and hope. These support meetings are very important since they provide opioid-dependent individuals with a safe and non-judgmental space to share their stories.

Addiction stigma is still very rampant in our society, and many people have a very disparaging attitude towards people who are addicted to drugs. This may discourage struggling drug addicts from seeking treatment. Through the twelve-step approach, the opioid-dependent patients are able to receive the treatment and support they need to go through rehabilitation and recover from their illness.

This strategy is based on the premise that people can help each other to achieve and maintain abstinence from opioid drugs. There are several emotional and mental transformative tools and techniques that the twelve-step approach aims to impart to opioid-dependent patients. These include:

- The ability to recognize their addiction problem as an illness.
- The awareness of addiction as a problem that exists, and one that requires outer intervention and aid.
- The practice of self-observation to become aware of the habits that gave rise to the addiction problem.
- Techniques to help one develop self-restraint and confidence in their ability to recover from addiction.

- Developing self-acceptance and the ability to overcome negative coping mechanisms.
- Cultivating compassion towards others who struggle with addiction and their affected families.
- Tools that foster continual recovery in the long run.

With the help of these tools and strategies, individuals are empowered to change habits that enable their opioid addiction and learn positive ones that can help them recover. Here are the twelve steps that are envisioned in this approach to addiction recovery:

1. Admit you are powerless over the addiction.
2. Have faith that a higher power beyond yourself can help you.
3. Make the decision to hand over control to this higher power.
4. Always keep a personal inventory.
5. Admit to yourself, to the higher power in charge and to the others in your group any wrongs you may have done.
6. Be willing to allow your errors to be corrected by the higher power.
7. Request the higher power to remove these shortcomings.
8. Create a list of all the wrong things you may have done against others and be willing to make amends.
9. Reach out to the people you may have hurt, unless it poses a risk to their health and wellness.
10. Continue keeping an inventory and acknowledge when you hurt others.
11. Try to connect with the higher power through meditation.
12. Share these strategies with others who may need

them.

In many rehabilitation centers, this twelve-step approach to addiction is often combined with evidence-based treatment that involves the use of medication. Although there are references to 'God' or a higher power in this twelve-step approach to treatment, this program is not religious. As a matter of fact, the higher power can be anything that you consider to be bigger than you.

The twelve-step approach to opioid addiction treatment and recovery provides a safe and supportive environment for recovering opioid addicts to share their experiences with others who have gone through similar struggles. In the structured therapy meetings, not only is knowledge imparted, but positive relationships are also forged. Twelve-step meetings can be found in many locations throughout the United States. Individuals who are in their early stages of recovery usually attend several meetings every week, although attendance is not always mandatory.

One of the most unique features of the twelve-step group therapy meetings is that they are typically led by individuals who have recovered from addiction instead of drug counselors. Participants are allowed and encouraged to share their experiences and perspectives with other members of their group. They are, however, strongly discouraged from speaking about the members' stories with outsiders. This ensures that the meetings maintain some level of confidentiality in order to ensure the privacy of participants is respected and upheld.

Research has shown that individuals who take part in the twelve-step approach generally tend to reduce their opioid use compared to those who do not go through this kind of therapy. Studies have also shown that early involvement in a twelve-step program can significantly increase the chances of successful long-lasting treatment.

Brief Motivational Interventions

Brief motivational interventions are short-term strategies that are put in place in order to help reduce the use of opioids by those who are dependent on them. These interventions usually entail two components namely:

- A thorough assessment of the quantity, frequency, and implications of drug use.
- Customized motivational strategies that are based on personal feedback and behavioral comparison.

Studies have shown that through a personal assessment of one's addictive actions, changes can be made to the manner in which one responds to one's urges and impulses. By gaining a deeper awareness of the risks involved in their drug use, individuals are able to develop a more balanced perspective, and effect changes that are required to stop using drugs.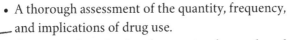

Apart from the assessment of one's habitual patterns, brief motivational interventions entail the use of one or more motivational improvement strategies. This approach is predicated on the idea that the cost of addictive habits must outweigh the benefits in order for an individual to be motivated enough to change.

Medication Management

In nearly all cases of opioid addiction, treatment often involves the use of medications like methadone and buprenorphine. These drugs are usually administered to patients to neutralize the effects of opioids and reduce withdrawal symptoms that may be experienced. The aim of medication management programs is to limit the use of the drugs gradually rather than engage complete abstinence, which often produces unpleasant withdrawal symptoms.

Longer-acting opioid drugs are usually administered in this addiction treatment strategy to prevent adverse withdrawal side effects that would be induced when the agonist drug is withdrawn.

Contingency Management

Contingency management is a type of intervention that is aimed at changing one's habits through certain incentives. The guiding principle behind this treatment approach is that people are more likely to repeat certain practises if they are enforced or rewarded. There are numerous incentives that can be used in this intervention to help fight addiction. These include low-value cash incentives, gift vouchers incentives, and clinic privileges.

Studies suggest that contingency management can be very effective when it comes to promoting positive practices to people who are struggling with opioid addiction. Nevertheless, this treatment strategy has also garnered a lot of criticism from clinicians. There are those who believe that this approach is unethical since it essentially involves bribing people in order to get them to behave in ways that are ultimately beneficial for themselves. Others have even argued that the use of rewards to motivate habitual change in opioid addicts may undermine their intrinsic motivations, thus jeopardizing treatment outcomes. Finally, there are those who have raised objections purely on financial terms. They argue that this approach is too expensive and unsustainable in the long run.

Despite these objections, many addiction therapists are beginning to employ this strategy in their arsenal when it comes to treating patients who suffer from opioid addiction. When combined with other treatment approaches, contingency management can go a long way in helping an opioid-dependent change habits that fuel their addiction.

Peer Support and Lifestyle Changes

Strong peer support is very crucial during the recovery period since it provides an anchor for the individual as they go through different treatment programs and strategies. Moreover, peers can offer guidance on the strategies to apply in order to minimize the risk of relapse.

The support of friends and relatives also plays an important role in the process of addiction recovery. Remember, addiction recovery is a life-long journey that requires a lot of patience and dedication. Unless an individual has people around them who are willing to support and care for them throughout the process, they may struggle with recovery.

Granted, living with a person who is dependent on opioids can complicate relationships by eroding trust and weakening communication. With the right support and care from close associates, people who struggle with opioid addiction can make great strides in their recovery journey. Here are some of the key ways in which the relatives and friends of recovering addicts can help them make progress in their fight against opioid addiction:

- Understand that the addiction treatment is not a quick fix, and there is a chance that the recovering patient might relapse multiple times.
- Create a healthy environment for the recovering individual by keeping the home drug-free.

- Become actively involved in the treatment and monitor the progress of the recovering patient.
- Try to learn about the recovering patient's stressors and triggers and minimize them where possible.

Dealing with a loved one's opioid addiction can undoubtedly be a very heart-wrenching experience. By providing them with the right support and being invested in their recovery, you can significantly increase their chances of achieving a complete recovery and living drug-free lives.

As we come to the end of this chapter, let us briefly recap some of the key pointers that we have discussed:

- Opioid addiction has a biological as well as mental component which must be considered when determining the right approach to treatment.
- There are several FDA-approved drugs that are crucial in the medicinal treatment of opioid dependence and addiction, including, methadone, buprenorphine and naltrexone.
- Successful treatment of opioid addiction requires a combined approach using various strategies which address the different elements that contribute to opioid dependency.
- Support from relatives, friends, and society as a whole can significantly increase the chances of individuals making a full recovery from substance abuse and addiction.
- Cognitive-behavioral therapy along with medical interventions are necessary strategies in addiction treatment since they help the recovering patient recognize and change the negative behaviors which contribute to their disease.

8

TMC AND OTHER NATURAL
TREATMENTS

M ost medical and behavioral interventions that are used for opioid addiction treatments are highly effective at helping individuals overcome the habit. These interventions do come with their fair share of side effects, most of which can be very difficult to contend with. The use of opioid antagonists like methadone, naloxone, and buprenorphine, for instance, produces withdrawal effects which are very unpleasant. In light of this, it is prudent to consider alternative pain-management treatments that are available in case you are struggling with opioid dependence and addiction.

In this closing chapter, we will investigate a number of alternative treatments for addiction, including traditional Chinese medicine, acupuncture and acupressure, herbs, essential oils, and flower essence. By the end of this topic, you will have all that you require in order to make the right choice when it comes to the most suitable supplemental treatments to boost your recovery.

Before we begin, let me reiterate that the strategies and

products outlined here should be used in conjunction with approved treatments for opioid addiction, as they are designed to help ease the transition from dependency to recovery by enhancing the physical and emotional state of the individual.

Traditional Chinese Medicine (TCM)

For thousands of years, traditional Chinese medicine has been used to treat a wide array of conditions, including mental illnesses and drug addiction. One of the concepts used to assess the problem of addiction is known as the 'empty flare,' which presupposes that the flaring up of behavioral and emotional symptoms of addiction is a result of the loss of a calm center. The treatment is designed to restore balance and nourish the Yin aspect in order to facilitate recovery.

TCM approaches to addiction treatment typically encapsulate the entire process of recovery from the time the problem is diagnosed to the time an individual has fully recovered from their drug dependence. This natural treatment strategy works to support the patient through the withdrawal process by helping to minimize the effects and reduce cravings. TCM aims to treat opioid addiction without the use of the antagonist drugs that are commonly employed in Western approaches to treatment.

Acupuncture and Acupressure

Acupuncture is one of the most common all-natural therapies that is employed in the treatment of opioid addiction as well as other health problems like back pain, fibromyalgia, and headaches. This technique was developed thousands of years ago and has since been adopted in many regions around the world. What is acupuncture and how is it used to treat addiction?

Acupuncture is a non-drug therapy that involves the stimulation of various body points using needles to relieve or eliminate physical and mental pain. Since the early 1970s, acupuncture has been an integral part of treatments designed to alleviate stress, anxiety, depression and drug addiction. It involves sticking needles into the bodies of patients to help ease the withdrawal symptoms that are associated with substance addiction. Studies have shown that patients who undergo this type of therapy in addition to other comprehensive treatments like psychological counseling, peer-group support involvement, and education experience a number of benefits, including reduced drug cravings, better quality of sleep, and relief from anxiety.

How effective is acupuncture when it comes to opioid addiction treatment? Numerous studies have been conducted to determine the success rate of acupuncture as a treatment for opioid dependence and addiction. In one particular study, auricular acupuncture was used to treat 82 patients struggling with cocaine addiction. The subjects were administered daily acupuncture treatment sessions for a period of two months. The findings showed that patients who received these treatments along with medical therapies using drugs like methadone were more likely to abstain from cocaine use compared to patients who were only treated with methadone.

Similar studies have been conducted on patients struggling with other forms of addiction, including alcohol and tobacco. The positive findings of these studies seem to suggest that acupuncture can be used in the treatment of opioid addiction. This treatment is most effective when combined with other therapies such as behavioral counseling and medical interventions.

In order to gauge the appropriateness of acupuncture for a patient's needs, it is important for the nature and structure of this treatment to be understood. This allows the patient to know what to expect with this type of therapy and prepare both physically and mentally for the treatment. The initial step in acupuncture treatment typically entails examining a person's health history, their timeline of addiction, and any underlying physical and mental illnesses. The therapist may also ask about any physical pain or stress that the patient may be experiencing.

Once the medical history of the patient has been established, the doctor will conduct a medical examination to establish the severity of their addiction before providing a referral to an acupuncture therapist. After the therapist has performed a thorough assessment of your physical and psychological health, they will prescribe a variety of acupuncture treatments to get rid of physical pain and make you more relaxed. Treatment typically entails inserting needles through various pressure points on the body. This procedure should be done slowly and carefully to minimize the potential for pain. Usually, the needles are left on the skin for between five to thirty minutes.

In some cases, the needles may need to be heated or twirled in order to maximize their effectiveness. Once the recommended therapy time has elapsed, the needles are carefully removed from the skin and ointment is applied to soothe the pain. The treatment may be administered several times a week depending on the needs of the patient.

Although acupuncture has been proven to be very beneficial in reversing the effects of drug use, it is not recommended as a single therapy for opioid addiction. This is mainly because recovering patients may still need to go through a medical detoxification process to boost their chances of full recovery.

Acupressure is a natural treatment technique which is very similar to acupuncture. Unlike acupuncture which involves the application of needles into specific parts of the body, acupressure generally involves the use of fingertips to manually apply pressure on key points. The application of acupressure is believed to help alleviate pain by stimulating the production of feel-good hormones known as endorphins. Consequently, acupressure can be used to manage chronic pain arising due to medical conditions such as menstrual cramps, muscle tension, nausea induced by chemotherapy, and many other illnesses.

The greatest benefits of acupuncture and acupressure in opioid addiction treatment lies in their ability to relieve pain and promote relaxation. These techniques can help alleviate the mental and emotional distress associated with opioid addiction. Hence, by combining them with other treatment options, the success rate for complete recovery can be significantly increased.

HERBS

Herbal therapies are often employed in the treatment of substance addiction and dependence. These treatments are not meant to be stand-alone addiction recovery therapies; they are used in conjunction with other treatment strategies to improve the success rate of addiction treatment. Some of the most popular plant-based medicines include:

Hawthorne Berries

Hawthorne berries have been shown to be highly beneficial

for hearts that have been weakened by prolonged substance abuse and eating disorders such as bulimia and anorexia. These berries are generally mild in their composition, and consequently pose no threat to individuals whose cardiovascular health has been undermined by prolonged opioid abuse.

It usually takes several weeks of daily use before the effects of this powerful natural herbal medicine become apparent. In case you prefer to avoid the alcohol-content in this herbal plant, you can simply put your dosage of the herb in boiling water for a few minutes. This will cause the alcohol composition to evaporate so that you are left with pure medicine.

Dandelion

Prolonged usage of opioid substances can cause significant damage to the spleen, which is responsible for protecting the body against infections and keeping body fluids in balance. Although this herb is safe to use, you should take extra caution, especially if you are suffering from gallstones.

Milk Thistle

Milk thistle is a strong herbal medicine that can help soothe the liver in case it has been damaged by continual opioid use. This herbal plant improves the ability of the liver to eliminate drugs and other harmful chemicals, thereby making it a highly beneficial medicine to include in any comprehensive addiction recovery plan. It should be noted that this herbal extract may induce mild diarrhea since it stimulates the production of bile but should not be a serious cause for concern. In case you experience this unpleasant side effect, you should simply take a break from the medicine until your bowel movements normalize, and then increase the dose gradually over time.

Burdock Root

Burdock root is a natural herb that acts as an anti-inflammatory agent, an antioxidant, and a blood purifier. It also functions as a diuretic by stimulating the body's release of excess water and flushing chemical compounds from the body through the kidneys. In addition to this, burdock root is also a nutritive herb that helps replenish the body with nutrients that may have been flushed out by dysfunctional kidneys.

Regular intake of burdock root allows your body to heal during the addiction recovery process, and should be a part of your daily herbal protocol. For best results, you may want to combine it with camomile, lemon balm, and basil.

MEDITATION THERAPY

Meditation is a very powerful and simple technique that has been proven to be highly effective in treating a wide array of mental and emotional health issues including depression, anxiety, and stress. In recent years, the practice of meditation has also been co-opted as a strategy for treating drug and substance addiction. Earlier on, we discussed some of the psychological implications of opioid abuse on mental health and saw the complex relationship of dual diagnosis disorders which encompass both drug addiction and mental illness. It is only logical, then, that treatments for addiction also envisage the mental wellbeing of people who are trying to recover from opioid addiction.

The aim of meditation therapy is to enable the individual to foster a sense of balance between their physical and mental states. Meditation techniques such as breathing exercises and mantra chants can help increase an individual's awareness and make them become more connected. Some of the characteristics which are commonly associated with all meditative practices include the lotus pose and controlled breathing exercises. There are various methods of meditation therapy that are designed to benefit individuals in specific ways. These include:

Mindfulness Meditation

This is the ability of an individual to be fully aware of what is going on within them as well as in their external environment without being overly reactive or overwhelmed. Individuals who are able to exercise mindfulness meditation are more capable of coping with the withdrawal symptoms of opioids without relapsing back to dependence and addiction. Moreover, it can help reduce anxiety and depression, providing recovering opioid users with the mental strength and fortitude that they require in order to completely give up the habit of substance abuse.

Zen Meditation

This is a form of meditation that is rooted in ancient Buddhist psychology and philosophy. The aim of this meditation method is to regulate an individual's attention through a practice known as "thinking about not thinking." Zen meditation usually requires practitioners to sit in a lotus position (with their legs crossed) and focus their attention inwards. Sometimes, it may also include controlled breathing exercises in which the practitioner keeps count of their inhales and exhales.

The practice of Zen meditation is quite similar to mindfulness meditation since it is aimed at cultivating a presence of mind. Unlike mindfulness, whose objective it is to focus one's attention on a particular object, Zen meditation is meant to foster general awareness. Individuals who practice this form of meditation are able to expand the scope of their attention and increase their awareness of their thoughts, emotions, and perceptions

Studies have shown that Zen meditation offers numerous cognitive, emotional and physical benefits to its practitioners. Apart from alleviating symptoms of stress and anxiety, it can also help recovering opioid addicts to become more connected and aware of their personal predispositions. This can influence them to let go of destructive thought patterns and actions that trigger their addictive tendencies and allow them to form positive thought and behavioral patterns that will catalyze their recovery.

Guided Meditation

Guided meditation is a form of relaxed meditative practice that is led by another person known as a teacher. The guide in this type of meditation can be a spiritual guru, yoga instructor or even a recorded CD. The role of the guide is to narrate the dynamics of the mind during meditation and instruct the individual on how to perform the meditation techniques.

If you are looking to start practicing this form of meditation therapy, you may need to enroll for a meditation class. If you live in a city or town where finding an instructor is difficult, there are various mobile apps that you can use to perform guided meditation by yourself in the comfort of your home.

There are plenty of benefits that guided meditation offers to those who practice. These include increased awareness, reduced negative thinking, and increased ability to cope with stressful situations and increased tolerance for pain and discomfort - this is particularly important for people who are trying to quit prescription opioids and adopt healthier ways of dealing with chronic pain. Guided meditation can also help those who are struggling with opioid addiction to become more mentally resilient in order to follow through with treatment despite the negative withdrawal effects that they may experience during abstinence.

Transcendental Meditation

This is a method of meditation that is aimed at cultivating and maintaining a state of relaxed awareness. During the practice of transcendental meditation, the practitioner is required to sit in a comfortable position with their eyes closed and recite a mantra that allows them to focus their concentration.

Through this process, the ordinary awareness of the individual is transcended, and they are able to achieve a state of pure consciousness or 'being.' At this point, the practitioner reaches a state of perfect stillness, stability, and order, unaffected by whatever bodily sensations or emotions they may be experiencing.

Transcendental meditation has been shown to offer impressive health benefits to those who pursue it. This form of meditation therapy can help reduce chronic pain, relieve anxiety and depression, improve immunity, and promote overall well being. Individuals who struggle with opioid addiction can greatly benefit from incorporating this therapy in whatever treatments they are already undergoing.

ESSENTIAL OILS

Essential oils have been shown to offer numerous benefits when it comes to addiction recovery. Although these products do not function as cures for addiction, they can provide a much-needed boost to one's mental health and promote overall wellness in the long run. Essential oils are usually employed in a treatment known as aromatherapy. Here are some of the ways in which the use of essential oils can improve the process of recovery from addiction:

- They help reduce withdrawal symptoms once an individual cuts on opioid use.
- They minimize anxiety and stress.
- They can improve one's mood.
- They induce relaxation and can help improve the quality of sleep.
- They help in alleviating chronic pain.
- They can significantly boost one's immune system.
- They can provide mental clarity and peace.

There are various essential oils that can be used in addiction recovery treatments, including:

Ginger Oil

This essential oil is usually extracted from the rhizomes of the ginger plant through a distillation process. It has a strong scent, spicy and warm. Ginger oil is commonly used in aromatherapy, and has been shown to have several benefits to its users, including alleviating headaches and providing relief from arthritis pain. It can also help soothe nausea, which is one of the main symptoms associated with opioid use and abuse.

Grapefruit Oil

Grapefruit oil is an orange-tinted essential oil, which is extracted from the peels of the grapefruit through a process known as cold-pressing. This citrus-scented oil is often used in aromatherapy thanks to the myriads of benefits that it offers. Grapefruit oil produces a calming effect on the body and mind, relieves anxiety and stress and lowers blood pressure. In addition to these health benefits, studies have shown that this essential oil also has mood stabilizing properties that can help reduce intense cravings. It is not surprising that many health and wellness experts often recommend Grapefruit oil to people who are trying to kick the habit of opioid use.

Bergamot Oil

Bergamot is an essential oil that is derived from the rinds of citrus fruits that grow on the Bergamot orange plant. This compound is highly prized for its natural sweet scent, and lends itself to a wide variety of applications. Bergamot oil is also known to produce a number of benefits including stress reduction, anti-inflammation, and pain relief.

The oil can be applied in various ways such as room diffusion and skin application. When used as an ointment, bergamot oil should be diluted with a carrier oil to prevent skin irritation.

TREATING OPIOID DEPENDENCE BY CORRECTING ELEMENTAL BALANCES

In Chinese Medicine, there are five natural elements in nature that correspond to the energies that move through the life force of an individual. These fundamental elements are wood, fire, metal earth, and water. It is thought that for an individual to be healthy, these elemental forces must be in balance. Each of the elements corresponds to or is associated with a particular energy point or body part. For instance, wood symbolizes the liver and gallbladder, fire represents the heart, earth is associated with the spleen, metal denotes the lungs, and water represents the kidneys.

When one or more of these elements are not balanced in the body, an individual may become prone to sickness. As a result, treatment is often aimed at restoring the balance of these crucial life forces. The diagnostic approach in this Traditional form of medicine is usually very thorough. In addition to conducting blood sugar and cholesterol tests, the medical practitioner may also ask the patient questions to determine their sensory experience. Depending on the symptoms presented, the doctor will then probe deeper to determine the elemental imbalance that is causing the symptoms

Treatment plans in this form of medicine are usually highly customized, and may include detoxification, clinical nutrition, and the use of Chinese medicinal herbs.

There are plenty of natural therapies that can be applied concurrently with clinical interventions when treating opioid addiction. Here are the main takeaways from this chapter on how these non-drug treatments should be applied:

- Traditional Chinese Medicine (TCM) therapies can be used to boost one's physical and mental resolve to quit opioid use, thereby increasing their chances of recovery.
- Acupuncture is very effective at treating chronic pain and can be applied as an alternative pain-relief treatment to prescription opioids.
- Various herbs such as Hawthorne berries and dandelions help reverse the effect of prolonged opioid use and facilitate faster recovery of organs that have been affected by addiction.
- Essential oils can help alleviate the serious

withdrawal effects that arise from opioid addiction, thus improving the chances of full recovery.

- All-natural treatments must be used in conjunction with medication therapies and psychological counseling in order to provide holistic treatment for opioid addiction.

AFTERWORD

Drug and substance abuse is without a doubt one of the biggest challenges that our society has been facing in recent history. The increased use of prescription opioids and similar illegal drugs has unwittingly given rise to a new drug crisis which we are far from solving. Policymakers have often asserted that drug addiction is a criminal matter that requires legal recourse to defeat it. Nevertheless, the failure of public policy to rein in opioid addiction is proof that we need to rethink our strategy if we are to defeat this enemy.

My aim for writing this book was two-fold. First, I wanted to give voice to a more objective perspective on addiction, based not only on anecdotal evidence but also on scientific case studies. The prevailing attitudes towards substance abuse and addiction have always been very reductionist and contemptuous. Individuals who struggle with drug addiction are always seen as weak-minded, and their suffering is usually chalked up to poor life choices. An even more cynical attitude presumes that those who are addicted or dependent on these substances actually take them simply because they enjoy doing so. This, however, is not only a false deduction but can actually be a very destructive mindset. We have seen how false perceptions such as these often fuel stigma against persons who are struggling with addiction and make it difficult for them to access the treatment they require in order to kick the habit.

The fact of the matter is that addiction is not a result of poor choices or weak will. On the contrary, it is a chronic illness that requires continual comprehensive treatment and care to overcome. We have seen how complex and multi-layered this illness is, in the sense that it not only affects one's physical health but can also have significant implications for a person's psychological state. To achieve full recovery, treatment should focus not only on restoring the physical health of the patient but also on improving their mental health so that they are able to abstain from drug use altogether.

My other objective for writing this book, which is perhaps more important, is to provide effective treatment strategies that can be employed in the fight against addiction. Due to a lack of information about the dynamics of this crisis, many people often wrongly assume that individuals who are dependent on drugs can quit using them if they simply decide to do so. This perception is very ill-informed, since it fails to account for actions that contribute to perpetual opioid dependence and addiction. We have seen how prolonged opioid use leads to changes in brain chemistry, which can alter not only one's mood but their ability to control and regulate their behavior. Obviously, there is an element of individual choice during the initial stage of opioid use. Once individuals develop tolerance and dependence, however, it can be very difficult for them to give up the use of opioids due to the adverse symptoms that are occasioned by withdrawal.

As such, the right treatment strategy should focus on helping the person gradually cut down on their opioid use until they reach a point of complete abstinence. Opioid antagonists like buprenorphine, methadone, and naloxone have been approved by the FDA for use in addiction treatment programs. These highly effective drugs are known to work by attaching to the brain's receptors in the same way that opioids do, thereby reversing the effects of agonists like morphine, codeine and heroin. Despite the effectiveness of these drugs, they may also produce unpleasant side effects, which can complicate treatment and make recovery much more difficult.

To improve the chances for successful recovery, these medical therapies should be combined with other strategies. One of the most important therapies that can be used together with medical interventions is psychological counseling. Since substance addiction often manifests together with mental illness in the form of a dual diagnosis, failure to employ holistic treatment for both conditions may lead to a cycle of addiction and poor mental health.

To slay the beast of dual diagnosis disorders, patients require behavioral therapy that trains them on how to identify the negative automatic thoughts that contribute to addictive practices. Behavioral therapy also enables recovering patients to learn positive coping mechanisms that can help them follow through with their treatment despite the challenging withdrawal symptoms that they may experience. In addition to the approved treatment strategies for addiction, there are a number of natural therapies that can be applied to alleviate the symptoms of addiction. These include Traditional Chinese Medicine and therapies such as acupuncture and acupressure, the use of herbs and essential oils as well as mental health therapies like meditation and yoga. While these natural methods do not single-handedly cure the illness, combined they can provide significant relief from the negative effects of opioid use and greatly boost the chances of full recovery.

We have also looked at the important role that support from peers and relatives play in opioid addiction recovery. Many individuals who struggle with opioid addictions often have very complicated relationships with their family members, friends, spouses, and community. They are often ostracized by the people closest to them, and this may take a serious toll on the victim's psychological state, and even trigger anxiety and depression.

On the other hand, when patients are provided with care, support and love, they are more likely to go through treatment successfully, and fully recover from their drug problem. To help our loved ones and friends to quit the habit of opioid use, it is vital that we invest our efforts towards their recovery, be patient with them, care for them, and support them throughout the process. Granted, living with a person who is recovering from opioid use can be psychologically and emotionally straining for the affected person. Persevering with them throughout the recovery process even when they relapse can lead to a better understanding of each other can in turn foster growth in relationships.

In conclusion, I would like to reiterate that although opioid addiction is a serious disease that can have negative effects on every aspect of one's life, it is not automatically a death sentence. Tens of thousands of people have been able to fully recover from opioid addiction, and have gone on to live productive lives. If you are struggling with substance addiction, you need not lose hope of recovery. With the right treatment, support and guidance, you too can kick the habit of opioid addiction and begin living a healthy and productive life once more.

In this book, I have painstakingly outlined answers to ending substance abuse and how to give up an opioid addiction. I have no doubt in my mind that you will find the wisdom contained herein very useful as you struggle to overcome the problem of addiction. In case you have loved ones who are trying to kick their opioid use, don't hesitate to share the knowledge you have received in this guide with them. You never know: it just might be the turning point that causes them to rethink their lives and make positive changes.

Finally, I would like to thank everyone who has been an invaluable help in the arduous yet very satisfying journey of writing this book. I do not underestimate the important insights that I have received from the respondents, experts, and patients that I have worked within the course of researching this subject. I would also like to thank you for choosing this book. I hope it has been an enjoyable and highly informative read. Kindly give us a review and share what you think about this book and what you have learned from it.

NEED HELP ??
HERE IS A LIST OF A FEW OF THE TOP TREATMENT
SPECIALISTS IN THE COUNTRY

THE LIST INCLUDES:

- *Nationally renowned treatment providers*
- *One-click linked portal access*
- *Locations and contact information*
- *Things to remember when seeking or providing help*

It's one thing to need help, and another to know where to go......

To receive your Renowned Treatment List, visit the link:

Renowned Treatment List

REFERENCES

A. (2017, December 11). Different Types and Causes of Substance Abuse - San Diego | API. Retrieved from https://apibhs.com/2017/12/11/types-causes-of-substance-abuse

Arjan, A. (2018, June 19). How Does Drug Addiction Affect Relationships? Retrieved from https://medmark.com/how-does-drug-addiction-affect-relationships/

Assistant Secretary of Public Affairs (ASPA). (2018, April 19). Treatment for Opioid Use Disorder and Addiction. Retrieved from https://www.hhs.gov/opioids/treatment/index.html

Body In Mind Archives. (n.d.). Retrieved April 26, 2020, from https://relief.news/category/body-in-mind/

Bueno-Gómez, N. (2017, September 29). Conceptualizing suffering and pain. Retrieved from https://peh-med.biomedcentral.com/articles/10.1186/s13010-017-0049-5

Butanis, B. (2018, April 30). What Are Opioids? Retrieved from https://www.hopkinsmedicine.org/opioids/what-are-opioids.html

Division, D. C. (2018, November 21). Prevention Programs & Tools. Retrieved from https://www.hhs.gov/opioids/prevention/prevention-programs-tools/index.html

Drug addiction (substance use disorder) - Symptoms and causes. (2017, October 26). Retrieved from https://www.mayoclinic.org/diseases-conditions/drug-addiction/symptoms-causes/syc-20365112

Drug, Alcohol Addiction: What are the Factors That Play a Role? (2020, March 5). Retrieved from https://emeraldcoastjourneypure.com/drug-alcohol-addiction-factors/

Felman, A. (2018, November 2). What are the treatments for addiction? Retrieved from https://www.medicalnewstoday.com/articles/323468#counseling-and-behavioral

Franchini, A. (2020, January 22). Opiate vs. Opioid – Do You Know the Difference? Retrieved from https://recoverycentersofamerica.com/blogs/opiate-vs-opioid-do-you-know-the-difference/

Genetics Home Reference. (n.d.). Opioid addiction. Retrieved April 26, 2020, from https://ghr.nlm.nih.gov/condition/opioid-addiction

Harvard Health Publishing. (2011, July 1). How addiction hijacks the brain. Retrieved from https://www.health.harvard.edu/newsletter_article/how-addiction-hijacks-the-brain

History of Pain: A Brief Overview of the 19th and 20th Centuries. (n.d.). Retrieved April 26, 2020, from https://www.practicalpainmanagement.com/treatments/history-pain-brief-overview-19th-20th-centuries

History of the Opioid Epidemic. (2018, August 16). Retrieved from https://dualdiagnosis.org/infographics/history-of-the-opioid-epidemic/

How opioid addiction occurs. (2018, February 16). Retrieved from https://www.mayoclinic.org/diseases-conditions/prescription-drug-abuse/in-depth/how-opioid-addiction-occurs/art-20360372

Juergens, J. (2019, December 6). Opiate Addiction, Abuse and Treatment. Retrieved from https://www.addictioncenter.com/opiates/

Lallanilla, M. (2006, January 6). A Brief History of Pain. Retrieved from https://abcnews.go.com/Health/PainManagement/story?id=731553&page=1

National Institute on Drug Abuse. (n.d.). A Letter to Parents. Retrieved April 26, 2020, from https://www.drugabuse.gov/publications/opioids-facts-parents-need-to-know/letter-to-parents

Northwestern Medicine. (2018, March 23). What You Need to Know About Opioids. Retrieved from https://www.nm.org/healthbeat/healthy-tips/what-you-need-to-know-about-opioids

Pain (Stanford Encyclopedia of Philosophy). (2019, March 4). Retrieved from https://plato.stanford.edu/entries/pain/

pubmeddev. (n.d.). Clonidine and naltrexone. A safe, effective, and rapid treatment of abrupt withdrawal from methadone therapy. - PubMed - NCBI. Retrieved April 26, 2020, from https://www.ncbi.nlm.nih.gov/pubmed/7138234

Stigma of Addiction | Reducing the Stigma of Substance Abuse. (2019, February 21). Retrieved from https://drugabuse.com/addiction/stigma/

TEDx Talks. (2018, November 26). The Stigma of Addiction | Tony Hoffman | TEDxFresnoState. Retrieved from https://www.youtube.com/watch?v=FuooVrSpffk

TEDx Talks. (2019, June 24). Shaming the Sick: Substance Use and Stigma | Dr Carolyn Greer | TEDxFortWayne. Retrieved from https://www.youtube.com/watch?v=eZ0CafocLsY

The Cause & Effect of Substance Abuse & Mental Health Issues. (2020, March 23). Retrieved from https://sunrisehouse.com/cause-effect/

The Neurobiology of Opioid Dependence: Implications for Treatment. (2002, July 1). Retrieved from https://www.ncbi.nlm.nih.gov/pmc/articles/PMC2851054/

The role of lifestyle in perpetuating substance use disorder: the Lifestyle Balance Model. (2020, April 26). Retrieved from https://www.ncbi.nlm.nih.gov/pmc/articles/PMC4326198/

What Are Opioids? - When Seconds Count. (n.d.). Retrieved April 26, 2020, from https://www.asahq.org/whensecondscount/pain-management/opioid-treatment/what-are-opioids/

What are the biggest misconceptions around addiction? (n.d.). Retrieved April 26, 2020, from https://www.drugrehab.com/addiction/stigma/

What causes addiction? (2018, November 2). Retrieved from https://www.medicalnewstoday.com/articles/323483#takeaway

What Causes Addiction? The Science of Drug & Alcohol Addictions. (2019, June 12). Retrieved from https://drugabuse.com/causes-of-addiction/

Wikipedia contributors. (2019, November 25). The body in traditional Chinese medicine. Retrieved from https://en. wikipedia.org/
wiki/The_body_in_traditional_Chinese_medicine

Wikipedia contributors. (2020, April 14). Pain theories. Retrieved from https://en.wikipedia.org/wiki/Pain_theories

Made in the USA
Coppell, TX
18 June 2020

28535376R00085